Make Your Place: Affordable, Sustainable Nesting Skills
written and illustrated by Raleigh Briggs

First published March 15, 2009

Second edition, May 10, 2018

ISBN 9781621061250

Distributed in the book trade by PGW

Raleigh Briggs lives in Seattle. She enjoys good times, DIY, and getting mail: letsgiveuptheghost@gmail.com

Microcosm Publishing
2752 N Williams Ave.
Portland, OR 97227
www.microcosmpublishing.com
503-232-3666

I'D RATHER BE READING BOOKS FROM
Microcosm Publishing.com
2752 N WILLIAMS AVE • PORTLAND, OR 97227

Chapters 1 and 2 of this book were originally distributed as zines, entitled *Herbal First Aid* and *Nontoxic Housekeeping*. You can still get them through Microcosm.

Names: Briggs, Raleigh, author.
Title: Make your place : affordable, sustainable nesting skills / Raleigh
   Briggs.
Description: Second edition. | Portland, OR : Microcosm Publishing, [2018] |
   Includes bibliographical references.
Identifiers: LCCN 2017033706 | ISBN 9781621061250 (paper-over-board)
Subjects: LCSH: Home economics. | Sustainable living.
Classification: LCC TX162.2 .B75 2018 | DDC 640--dc23
LC record available at https://lccn.loc.gov/2017033706

Table of Contents

Introduction

When Make Your Place was first published, I always had to hunt for it in bookstores. (Yes, I look for my own books. I am complicated and imperfect.) It is a stubborn, genre-resisting book, and it must have been a pain for booksellers to shelve. Sometimes I'd discover it looking small and scrappy next to the glossy self-help books; sometimes it would be nestled like a sprout amongst the cookbooks or gardening manuals. How times have changed! Today, there are whole shelves of DIY books, and the Internet is lousy with clever "hacks" for things even I would never think to make myself.

And yet, my little sprout-book is still here, and still in print. To this day I get emails from all over the world. I go to new friends' houses for the first time, only to find a copy of Make Your Place on their shelf. Even with hundreds of titles to choose from, people continue to connect with my short, weirdly spaced, handwritten book. ♡ I am utterly humbled and deeply honored. ♡

But of course, I didn't invent this. I am just a conduit. Every bit of knowledge in the DIY world (and in this book) was passed down from folks who, because of their class, race, or gender, had to find a way to survive without the privilege of money and resources. We must honor that. This has been on my mind a lot in the ten years (WHAT) that this book has been in the world: how important it is to celebrate the ingenuity of DIY while being critical of the system that made it necessary in the first place. I hope you'll read with that intent, whether you're new to this book or just revisiting it.

It can be beautiful and freeing to create a life for yourself with your own hands, but we cannot stop there. How can we use these skills to build each other up? How can we extend that beauty and freedom to everyone, whether they share our privileges or not?*

*And especially if they don't!

That's my dream for the next leg of this little book's journey. Because if DIY frees us, it's gotta free all of us.

Thank you so, so much for reading. I hope you enjoy. ♡

Much love and gratitude,

(Raleigh Briggs, Seattle, August 2017)

Note the zine archive where this book was conceived, Seattle's Zine Archive and Publishing Project (ZAPP), has gone to the great free copy shop in the sky. Its absence has left a sizable hole in my heart. So I dedicate this book to the decades of ZAPP coordinators, volunteers, and patrons: you made that place, that mad scientist's lab of dreams and ideas, my very first home in my adopted city. None of this would have been written without you.

safety protocols

In this book, I've tried my best to include only recipes made with safe or safeish ingredients; however, like your favorite animal, even natural formulas can hurt you if you disrespect them. That said, here are some things to keep in mind:

Protocol 1: Natural ≠ Edible

Even though compounds like borax and washing soda are far safer than most of the ingredients you'll find lurking in your local drugstore, they shouldn't accidentally get inside your body. Same goes for essential oils, which are far too potent to use internally. Wash your hands after mixing cleaners and label the containers you keep them in. If you have sensitive skin, wear gloves when you clean.

Protocol 2: Wildcraft with Care

I am confident that everyone reading this knows not to carelessly pull plants out of the ground and eat them. Still, it bears repeating that if you wildcraft food and herbs, you need to do your research. A lot of communities offer free **or** low-cost wildcrafting workshops. Check out local parks departments, agricultural nonprofits, community colleges, and punk houses or co-ops. At the very least, get yourself a full-color field guide with large photos, and when you do find something foragable, collect it in a respectful and responsible way.

Protocol 3: Think of the Unborn Children!

If you're pregnant, please avoid the following essential oils and herbs:

clary sage   calendula   sage
juniper   camphor   St. John's Wort
cinnamon   comfrey   thyme
cedarwood   lemon balm   wintergreen
clove   neem   basil
anise   pennyroyal   myrrh

Protocol 4: Know Your Body

This, I think, is most important: if something makes you feel gross, or itchy, or you'd really rather take a pill, listen to your gut and do what is best for your terrifically free and unique body. This book is about making your life better, not about being hardcore.

Protocol 5: Plants Have Families

You know that botanical horror called ragweed? It's related to both calendula and chamomile. So if you have a ragweed allergy, avoid using any herb related to ragweed for cosmetic or medicinal purposes. Sorry.

chapter 1

Health + First Aid

Whenever I get into conversations about DIY I find that certain ideas get echoed by many different people. Chief among these tenets is the idea that DIY is about making even the tiny bits of our lives intentional: we focus our energy on what we know is right for us, rather than what is dictated by a market or culture. I think herbal medicine and DIY healthcare are such a strong manifestation of this idea. There is definitely a place for conventional medicine — it saves lives, after all. It's quick and effective and familiar. But it has the unfortunate effect of distancing us from our bodies. Instead of questioning why we have constant digestive issues, for example, we end up just tossing pills down our gullets like we're balancing the pH of a swimming pool. It's cold and isolating, not to mention expensive.

Compare this to the practice of using herbs, which work in a broader, less symptom-focused way. In the DIY healthcare mindset, you would tone a weak GI tract and strengthen it, rather than dulling it with antispasmodics. Natural medicine often takes time, but within that time there is an invitation to actually witness your body changing. It forces you to pay attention to the systems of your body, and how they interact and signal each other. Over time, we become less afraid of our mysterious guts and tunnels, and thus, more confident in our ability to heal ourselves. And that's what this chapter is all about!

a Quick Guide to
Essential Oils

Always use pure essential oil when you're making cleaners or remedies. Don't use anything labeled "perfume oil" or "aromatherapy oil." Essential oils can retain some of the antimicrobial, antibacterial, and antiviral properties of the whole plant. These oils are highly concentrated and volatile, so keep them in dark glass bottles away from direct sunlight and heat. And DO NOT EAT THEM. !

Here are some oils that come in handy:

· <u>Antibacterial</u>: bay, camphor, cardamom, chamomile, citronella, cypress, eucalyptus, ginger, hyssop, juniper, lavender, lemon, lemongrass, lemon verbena, lime, marjoram, orange, pine, rosemary, sage, sandalwood, spearmint, tea tree, thyme

· <u>Antimicrobial</u>: bergamot, chamomile, clove, eucalyptus, hyssop, lavender, lemon, lime, myrtle, nutmeg, oregano, patchouli, tea tree

· <u>Antiviral</u>: cinnamon, eucalyptus, lavender, lemon, oregano, sandalwood, tea tree, thyme

*NOTE: Please please please read the section on Safety before you use oils. It's important to me.

How-tos – basic recipes for salves, tinctures, and sundry curiousities

The following recipes are a good starting point for any budding (har!) herbalist. One small note : if you have the funds and the space available, I would recommend keeping a set of cooking tools exclusively for the purpose of making herbal remedies. Ideally this will include:

- an enamel or stainless steel pan, double boiler, or slow cooker
- a funnel
- cheesecloth or coffee filters
- a mortar + pestle (...or a plastic bag and a trusty cudgel)
- dark glass jars and bottles - use the kind with droppers if you are making tinctures, and fatter, wider jars with twisty lids for salves
- larger glass jars (jam + pickle jars are excellent) with tight-fitting lids, for steeping and soaking herbs
- a stirring utensil

making tinctures

A tincture is basically a combination of an herb and an appropriate solvent that is allowed to steep for several weeks. The result is a highly concentrated solution that captures the healing properties of the plant.

Tinctures are awesome because they're easy to make, portable, and if you make and store them properly, they'll stay potent for quite a while. They can be used to soak gauze for compresses, combined with creams or oils, or taken internally at a ratio of 30 or so drops in one glass of water, juice or tea.

To make a tincture, chop up a cup of whatever herb or herbs you are using (roots or woody stems should be dried and ground in a mortar and pestle). It is <u>very</u> important that you use dried herbs when you make salves + tinctures — the water in fresh herbs can harbor bacteria that will ruin your work. (Either lay herbs flat to dry or tie into small bundles and hang somewhere dry and sunny. To rig up a quick herb drying rack, secure herbs to a metal coathanger with some clothespins, and hang near a window or radiator)

Take your chopped herbs or roots and place them in a clean jar with a tight-fitting lid — a pickle or mayonnaise jar works great, just make sure it's a big'un. Cover the herbs with 5 cups of cheap 60 proof vodka; for a non-alcoholic version with some added health benefits, use apple cider vinegar. Seal up your jar and hide it from your friends in a cool, dark place. Let it sit there for two weeks, and give it a good shake every once in a while. When the two weeks are up, line a funnel

see?

fig. A

with several layers of cheese-cloth and strain the tincture into dark glass bottles. Pull the corners of the cheesecloth into a nice package and squeeze out any liquid before tossing the solids.

Cap your tinctures tightly, make some cute labels for them and keep them away from heat and light.

Ta DAH!

*making infusions, * decoctions + poultices

An <u>infusion</u> is a quantity of water or other liquid in which herbs have been steeped long enough for the properties of the herbs to transfer to the water. Usually, the water is first boiled, and then poured over the plant matter. Yes, this is pretty much the same thing as tea; in fact, I will use the words "tea" and "infusion" interchangeably in this book. To make an infusion, boil one cup of water for every teaspoon or so of dried leaves, soft stems, or flowers (we'll get to bark + roots in a second). If you're using fresh herbs, make sure to wash them well, and double the amount you're using. Pour the boiling water down over the herbs, cover and let steep until cool. The best way to do this is in a mason jar. For stronger infusions, use more herbs or let the jar sit for longer. When steepage is complete, strain out all the plant material, transfer to a clean jar, and refrigerate what you don't use right away.

Decoctions are a lot like infusions, but making them involves boiling the herbs and water together. This method is used for woody stems, bark and roots. Combine 1 oz herb with a quart of water and boil, covered, for 20 minutes. From there, follow the instructions for making infusions.

A poultice is basically a pulp made of herbs, and sometimes other ingredients, that is applied directly to the skin to treat swelling, bites, and so on. To make a poultice, grind fresh herbs until juicy and/or sticky. If you're dealing with dryish plants, moisten the mixture with a little clean water, or better yet, an herbal infusion or decoction.

Infused oils can be used for massage, skin and hair care. Bruise a handful of fresh herbs by rolling them between your hands, and stick them in an airtight bottle filled with your favorite carrier oil. I like almond, grapeseed, and cheap (not extra virgin) olive oils. Cap the bottle tightly and keep it in a cool, dark place, like a kitchen cupboard. Shake it once and a while and strain out the herbs after a week or so.

making salves

Salves seem intimidating, but they are surprisingly easy to make, and they're pretty impressive when they're finished. Salves protect and nourish the skin while it's healing. You can make salves by stewing herbs in oil and adding beeswax as a thickener and skin protectant. You can also use infused oils you've already made. For equipment, you'll need an enamel or glass pot, a wooden spoon, and a grater.

Salve A: Infused-Oil Method

2 oz infused oil
2 T grated beeswax
2 drops essential oil (optional)

Warm the oil over low heat until just hot. Add the beeswax and stir the mixture until all the wax is melted. Add the oil if you're using it.

Pour the mixture into a small glass jar and let it cool. At this point it should be solid. If it's too solid, reheat the salve and add another drizzle of oil. If it's too soft, reheat and add more wax. When it's the right consistency, pour it back into the little jar, cap it tightly, and label it.

Salve B: Stewed-Herb Method

2 oz dried herbs

1 cup (8 fl. oz) olive oil

1 oz beeswax (will vary according to how soft you want your salve to be), grated

Place the herbs and oil in an enamel pot, bring to a low heat (not a boil) and stew the herbs until the oil is dark green with herby juices (up to 3 hours) Stir occasionally. Strain out the herbs through two layers of cheese-cloth and return the oil to the pot. Add the beeswax and stir until totally melted. Pour the salve into wee jars and let cool.

Variation: After the salve is cooked, beat it for a minute or so with an electric mixer or an egg beater, to make a creamier salve.

You can also try stewing your herbs and oil in a slow cooker set to low, for 8-10 hours.

Vegan Alternatives to Beeswax include soy wax, carnauba wax and candellilia wax. You'll have to experiment with the proportions of wax to oil, as these waxes behave differently than bees-wax. Carnauba wax, for example, is much harder. You might also try melting some virgin coconut oil, which is solid at room temperature, and infusing it, then letting it resolidify. Keep the oil in a cool, dark place, especially in the summer.

* anatomy * of an herbal * first aid * kit *

Here are some basic remedies and hardware to stock in a good first aid kit. This is a big list, so feel free to tailor it to your lifestyle. For example, if you spend a lot of time outdoors, pack a poison ivy remedy and some aloe vera, and cut back on tinctures for headaches, etc.

tinctures for headaches, insomnia, stomach problems, and pain

salves, poultices and some aloe for sunburn, rashes, bruises + skin irritations

a wee bit of styptic

teas + infusions for cramps, nausea

a good, all-purpose healing + antiseptic salve or tincture

a couple of useful essential oils, like tea tree or lavender

TEAM: DIY!

bandages, surgical tape + gauze

small scissors

quarters (for phone)

single-edged razor blades (wrapped, please)

tweezers

eye cup or shot glass

latex gloves

energy bar or small bit of high-calorie food (non-perishable)

a bandana, to use as a sling or tourniquet

TEAM: ACCESSORIES

ALL OVER HEALTH TONICS

... because some herbs are so great you'll want to take them every day.

Burdock root is used as a vegetable in Japan. It's also a great tonic for the liver, skin, bladder, and blood. The fuzzy burrs of the burdock plant are the inspiration for Velcro! To use burdock, make a decoction with the root, or chew a fresh hunk of root.

It sucks that **nettles** are so jabby and despised, because they're actually AWESOME. Nettles are high in protein, iron, and vitamins. You can buy dried nettles and make tea, but you can also wildcraft them and eat them like spinach. To pick nettles, wear gloves, strip off young, tender leaves, and boil, steam or sauté them to get rid of those stingers!

Astragalus root is an immune system tonic that's especially important in traditional Chinese medicine. Like Echinacea, it's popular during cold + flu season. You can take astragalus on its own, but most prefer to combine it with other herbs they like, such as nettles or chamomile.

Damiana is a small Central American shrub that smells kind of like chamomile. Why do you care? Because it's an aphrodisiac! GO FOR IT!!

CUTS + SCRAPES

Firstly, some friendly advice: the following remedies are really for **mild** cuts, scrapes + irritations. If you gash yourself up really good please do not pour cayenne in it. It will suck. Anyway:

• Use the aforementioned cayenne, in powder form, as a styptic – aka a blood-clotting agent. Sprinkle a little right on the cut or scrape. It does smart a bit, though – you can also use comfrey or yarrow.

• Tea tree oil is a powerful antimicrobial agent. Dilute several drops of tea tree oil in a couple tablespoons of oil (almond or grapeseed oil is nice, but olive or vegetable oil works fine too) and apply to cuts, abrasions, fungal infections and skin irritations.

• Whip up an all-purpose healing salve for your various injuries and skin problems. Some good herbs to use for their soothing, antiseptic, and painkilling properties: comfrey, calendula, meadowsweet, goldenseal, marshmallow and horsebalm. Direct your attention to page 14 for instructions for making salves.

* NOTE: You can also make a tincture with any or all of the above herbs and apply to the skin as a wet compress with a dry bandage on top. *

ACHES & PAINS

Arnica is a lovely, yellow-bloomed member of the sunflower family that has been used for centuries to treat sprains, bruises, and muscle aches. While you should not take arnica internally, feel free to distill it into a tincture, use the flower heads in a salve, or mash them up and apply as a poultice to a sprained ankle. A quick compress for bruises and swelling can be made by soaking some clean gauze with arnica tincture and applying it to your (unbroken) skin. If you have sensitive skin or allergies, dilute the tincture with water, or use arnica infusion.

Arnica flowers also work well as part of a blend: for an excellent muscle salve, use equal parts arnica, witch hazel, and St. John's Wort. This formula is nice, because unlike a lot of commercial formulas that are supermentholated, it soothes your muscles without making you feel like your skin is on fire. But if you like that feeling, turn the page!

20 For a headier-smelling concoction with a bit of a tingle to it, combine an appropriate carrier oil (more on that in a minute) with a couple drops each of camphor, eucalyptus, rosemary, and clove bud oils. These essential oils are cooling and antiseptic; camphor and clove also have mild analgesic properties when applied topically. Shake your new massage oil well and rub into sore or tired muscles.

When you're making oils for your skin, it's important to choose an oil with the right consistency for your intended purpose, and one that's not too greasy. For massage, almond oil is always nice, and grape-seed oil is a good alternative for oilier skin. You can also try coconut oil — coconut oil is great for the skin, and is solid at room temperature, making it more portable. Just be sure it's melted when you mix in your essential oils. You can do this by placing your jar of oil in a big bowl of very hot water.

NOTE: Even though it's cheap, resist the temptation of mineral oil (baby oil). That "mineral" is petroleum, and that's what the oil feels like: gross, gloppy, and pore-clogging as all get out. Nast.

Burns, Rashes and skin conditions

Ahem: the following remedies work great for mild burns and sunburns. If you've burnt a large area of your body, or you've got chemical or electric burns, *for the love of God go to the ER.* And I hope you're okay.

Anyway, so you've burned yourself: your first course of action should be to cool your burnt skin under a cold tap or in an ice bath. Immediate cold will help prevent further injury, and in those first moments it will lessen your pain a great deal. While you're sitting there, drink a glass or two of cool water. Dehydration is a serious side effect of burns and sunburns, and not a lot of people realize how quickly it can set in.

DO! NOT! PUT GREASE! ON A BURN! That includes stuff like butter and petroleum jelly. Any oil will effectively trap heat against your skin, which is really the last thing you want. An oil barrier will also hinder air circulation and proper drainage, both of which are crucial to healing.

Now I am contractually obligated to talk about aloe vera. Just kidding! I will blab about aloe willingly, earnestly, joy-fully. It really is the best thing to use on any type of burn. On top of that, aloe is easy to grow and process yourself. To make DIY aloe gel, puree a couple handfuls of peeled aloe leaves with 150 IU of Vitamin C powder. Vitamin C is a natural preservative like Vitamin E and jojoba oil -but without the oil. Store your gel in the fridge - it keeps longer and feels nicer that way.

Other herbs that are good for burns include calendula, comfrey, chamomile, St. John's wort and plantain. If you have the essential oils of any of these plants, mix a few drops with some aloe gel (homemade, of course). Alternately, make a strong infusion with any or all of the above herbs, let it cool completely, and either apply as a compress or add to a cool bath. Whatever you do, <u>don't</u> use tinctures on burns. Tinctures are drying, and if you put them on burnt skin, it feels like you're soaking a hangnail in acetone - oh man, it hurts so bad. So don't do it!

For other skin ailments, like eczema and dermatitis, calendula and marshmallow are always good options. Either stew the herbs into a salve, use their infusions as a body splash or bath additive, or add a couple dropperfuls of tincture to some natural, unscented hand cream. Soap made with calendula petals is also nice.

Poison Ivy, Nettle, Etc.

A lot of folks swear by the inner flesh of the spotted jewelweed plant as a remedy for poison ivy. Jewelweed grows rampant all over the East Coast of North America. Look for it growing in wet environments, like creek beds. To use it, grab a stem and split it open. Rub the juicy inside of the stem over your rash.

For those of us in the West and beyond, plantain (the herb, not the fruit) is an excellent alternative. Different species of plantain grow all over the world, and many of these thrive as weeds in urban areas. To calm itching and pain associated with stings, rashes and skin

Calendula

irritations, crush or chew fresh plantain leaf and stick the resulting cud on the affected area.

✭ basic healing poultice powder

This is a basic formula for an all-purpose skin powder. It's good for blistered feet, small cuts, and when mixed with water to form a paste, is very soothing to rashes and insect bites...

- 1 part dried plantain
- 1 part goldenseal root
- 1 part dried marshmallow
- 1 part dried calendula

Grind everything into a fine powder using a coffee grinder, and keep in a plastic zip-top bag.

...and speaking of bug bites!

Tinctures of witch hazel, plantain, grindelia, comfrey, and St. John's wort are itch relievers. Add some to a bit of oil or lotion for a lone bite, or add diluted tincture (or infusion) to your bathwater. Lavender oil, diluted in a bit of almond oil, is also good for bites. And while you're in the tub, throw in a handful of baking soda, another great bite remedy.

To repel bugs, combine one, some, or all of the following essential oils in a base of vegetable oil (or equal parts vodka and water), and store in a spray bottle. Don't use more than 20 or so drops of essential oil altogether:

- ★ lavender ★ citronella ★ eucalyptus ★
- ★ cedarwood ★ lemongrass ★

Bite + Sting Plaster

This is like a tiny face mask for your bug bites. It's especially good for treating stings from bees, wasps, and yellow jackets.

> 1 part tincture of plantain (you can also use echinacea or comfrey)
> 1 part pure water (distilled)
> 1 part kaolin or bentonite clay (an astri--ngent clay that is usually available in bulk at co-ops and via mail order)
> A few drops of lavender essential oil (max 3)

Mix the ingredients together in a small bowl. Tweak the dry-to-wet ratio until the resulting paste is smooth and tacky enough to adhere to your skin. Mound a small bit of plaster on top of the bite and let it dry, at which point you can wash or rub it off.

This plaster will keep in an airtight container, but only for a little while. Try making a batch right before a picnic / hayride / kid's birthday party or other bug-friendly event.

Bruises, Bleeding, and other "Sports Injuries"

Arnica and comfrey are the first herbs you should reach for when you've got a bruise. Start by making an infusion of one or both plants and letting it cool. Then, either use the tea as a wet compress, or freeze it in ice cube trays, wrap the ice in a tea towel and apply to the bruise (don't use a plastic bag — you want the tea to wash over the bruise as it melts). The ice method is preferred whenever the bruise is accompanied by swelling.

Nosebleeds

If your nose bleeds often, keep on hand a bottle of yarrow tincture. Yarrow is a natural styptic and will help stop bleeding. Fold a length of clean fabric until it fits over the bridge of your nose, soak it in a combination of one teaspoon yarrow tincture and one cup water, and press the compress firmly over your nose.

Please do not eat me. I am for external use only.

arnica

Lean forward and let your head rest between

your knees. Try to relax and breathe deeply through your mouth. Make another compress with the yarrow tincture and place it across the back of your neck. With your free hand apply pressure to your upper lip.

PARASITES

If you've ever had head lice, you know that the treatment is this vile, burning shampoo that is just as awful as having lice. Essential oil of thyme is an effective herbal alternative because thyme is very high in phenol, an antiseptic and anti-parasitic chemical compound that's also present in other plants, like tea tree. To treat lice, add four drops of thyme oil in an ounce or two of olive oil and rub it in to your scalp. Put on a shower cap and relax for a half hour. Wash your hair with soap or shampoo and then comb the nits (tiny lice eggs) out with a very fine-toothed nit comb. Make sure you get every last nit - they look like little white dots clinging to your hair shaft. In the meantime, wash your sheets in the hottest water you can procure, and add some thyme oil to your laundry soap Oh yeah - you can treat crabs this way too.

*CAUTION: IF YOU ARE PREGNANT, DON'T USE THYME - JUST SHAVE YOUR HEAD

the fungus among us

Fungal infections can occur in several different areas of the body: athlete's foot, jock itch, ringworm, yeast infections and thrush are all types of fungal infection. They all suck pretty bad. Fortunately, most are quite easy to treat.

The first thing you should do to fight off a fungus is to increase the friendly bacteria in your body by taking some probiotics. These are found naturally in cultured products like yogurt and kefir (look for "active" or "live cultures" on the label), but you can find extracted probiotics like acidophilus in pill form too. For yeast infections, use yogurt (*plain* yogurt) topically in and around your genitals — use a little spoon or a tampon applicator to get it in there. Wear a pad afterwards while the yogurt's leaking out. Another remedy is to wrap a peeled clove of garlic in some cheesecloth, dip it in olive oil and insert it into the vagina You can tie a string around it for easy removal. Change the clove 3 times a day. If you'd rather avoid putting stuff inside you, or if you don't have a vagina, eating lots of yogurt and garlic can also be effective.

External infections, like athlete's foot, can be treated with antifungal herbs like tea tree oil. Here's a simple ointment that you can use all over:

1 cup olive oil
big handful calendula petals
10 drops tea tree oil

Infuse the calendula in the oil for a few days, then add the tea tree oil. Keep the ointment in a tight-lidded jar. Use as a massage oil on the infected area a couple times a day. If you have dandruff or a scalp infection, rub the ointment into your scalp, pull on a kerchief or shower cap, and sleep on it. Wash the oil out in the morning.

Antiseptic + Antifungal Soap

Use this on your hair and body

8 oz liquid castile soap, unscented
10 drops tea tree oil
5 drops lavender essential oil
5 drops eucalyptus essential oil

Add the oils to the soap and mix well. Store in a squeeze bottle.

More tricks:

• For especially itchy infections, like yeast infections, try soaking in a bath with a few handfuls of baking soda tossed in.

• Paint gentian violet tincture on any fungal infection. For yeast, soak a tampon in the solution. Make sure to wear a pad, because the stuff is purple.

• If your feet burn and itch, get someone to rub them with aloe vera gel with a couple drops of tea tree oil added in.

GUT PROBLEMS

Digestive issues can be either acute or chronic, and they are always pretty sucky. Fortunately, there are herbs out there that can work as digestive tonics that strengthen your GI tract, which makes it easier for you to manage a chronic condition. Among these, the most accessible is chamomile. Awesome, right? Because you already _like_ chamomile!

A strong cup of chamomile tea, taken three times a day, can tone a weak set of guts over time. Soothing.

For digestive complaints, I always prefer teas to tinctures, which are alcohol-based and can irritate an uppity stomach. If you've got the runs, check out raspberry leaf, blackberry leaf, slippery elm, and cranesbill. Let your herbs steep 10-30 minutes and drink a few cups, or until you're feeling better. In the meantime, make yourself a bowl of cooked white rice, avoid any foods that you know irritate your stomach, and make sure to drink lots of water to counteract dehydration.

If you just barely ate something really gross and a cold dread is creeping up your esophagus, reach for some charcoal tablets — tablets, not briquettes! **UGH**

The charcoal is incredibly absor-bant and will help to soak up your warm mayonnaise or whatever the hell that was. Follow the directions on the bottle, or take one or two tablets every four hours.

BARF! For nausea + motion sickness, try ginger, every-one's favorite rhizome. You can buy ginger powdered in tablets, but candied ginger is much tastier. You can buy it in bulk at most co-ops, health food stores, and Asian groceries.

Herbal teas are also helpful if you're backed up — try yellow dock, milk thistle, senna, and cascara sagrada. A cup of yerba maté tea, taken on an empty stomach, can also speed things up.* In between cups of tea, stick to a diet nigh in fiber, and try to move around a little. And yes, prunes will help you — a *lot*.

*Avoid this if you're sensitive to caffeine, or have ulcers **PLUHHHH**

Cold & Flu

There are so many herbs that fight colds, I'm just going to list them:

- Echinacea
- Boneset
- Goldenseal
- Garlic
- Usnea

Antimicrobial herbs that work to kill infections in the body and support the immune system

- Valerian
- Cramp Bark
- Passionflower

Antispasmodics for cramps and body aches

- Meadowsweet
- Slippery Elm
- Raspberry Leaf

Help reduce mucus secretions

- Elder Flower
- Peppermint
- Yarrow

Herbs that induce sweating, for reducing fevers

- Comfrey
- Colts foot
- Mullein
- Marshmallow
- Licorice

Expectorants, to help you cough it up

- Catnip
- Hops

mild sedatives, for better rest

* I recommend making a big thermosful of tea using a few of these herbs. Keep it next to your bed so you don't have to keep getting up to make tea. This also helps you to stay hydrated. Here's a good general cold/flu formula:

Cold & Flu Tea

¼ c each:
 Elder flowers
 Licorice
 Boneset

⅛ c Meadowsweet

⅛ c Catnip

2 T each:
 Peppermint
 Cramp Bark

Store in an airtight jar. Use one tablespoon herbs for every cup of water.

Mullein Ear Oil

Mullein is an anti-inflammatory, and a traditional herb for earaches.

• Combine in a small jar a handful of dried mullein flowers and a clove of sliced garlic (optional). Cover the herbs with olive oil, cap the jar, and let it sit in a sunny spot for a few days. Strain out the flowers and transfer the oil to a dropper bottle. Use 2-3 drops in your achey ear once or twice a day. Warm it up first if you like—just stick it in your pocket for a minute.

Sinus Wash

One of the simplest ways to treat congestion is to irrigate your sinuses with a saline solution. Use a neti pot or a cup to pour this mixture gently into one nostril and let it drip out the other. Refill the pot and repeat on the other side, and then gently blow your nose. Use ⅛ t sea salt to every cup of warm water, and add a pinch of baking soda.

Herbal Eye Wash

Eyebright. Guess what it does!

Make an infusion with one cup of water plus ½ teaspoon each:

> eyebright
> goldenseal root
> red raspberry leaf

Strain it <u>very</u> well and use it with an eye cup or shot glass to help soothe tired eyes or fight eye infections.

mouth & tooth issues

Oil of clove is an important ingredient in a lot of dental products, including crowns (if you've ever had a root canal: oil of clove is why your crown sometimes smells improbably like perfume). Clove oil has strong antiseptic and painkilling properties, and can be found in most drugstores, in the pharmacy section next to the other "olde tyme apothecary" stuff. Put a drop on a cotton swab or bit of dental floss, and apply to your aching tooth, making sure not to swallow any.

Thyme is another herb with a stellar reputation for killin' germs. You can use a strong tea or diluted thyme tincture as a mouth rinse to clean mouth wounds and lessen your chances of infection.

If you are completely bereft of all healing plants, make a solution of warm water and sea salt. Sea salt is naturally astringent and is perfect for gently cleansing tissue that's healing from trauma. Sea salt solution works to temporarily soothe sore throats, also.

PMS

+ MENSTRUAL ISSUES!

I've always had the kind of blitzkrieg PMS that seems to assault every organ in my body at the same time. Maybe you also have this problem.

To counteract a number of different symptoms, make a tea blend with the following and drink 2-3 cups a day:

2 T dandelion root — diuretic to help swelling and/or bloating. Also full of iron + nutrients

2 T chamomile
2 T lemon balm — calming, for emotional support

2 t raspberry leaf
2 t cramp bark — antispasmodics to soothe cramps

2 t fresh ginger — aids digestion and is tasty

Valerian is also excellent for stopping cramps — since it's also a sedative, it's best used to treat nighttime cramps, or cramps you have when you know you aren't going to do anything productive. You can also take cramp bark tincture, which is quite effective.

If you're bloated and uncomfortable, make sure to drink lots of water and herbal tea. If you can find young dandelion greens to eat, they are super nutritious and will help flush out retained fluid. Avoid coffee- even though it makes you pee, it doesn't help with water retention. Ain't that a kick in the ass?

36 If you have ongoing menstrual troubles like erratic periods, painful periods or especially heavy bleeding, try drinking red raspberry leaf tea as a uterine tonic. Drink a cup or two a day, and add an extra cup when you're menstruating, to help with cramps.

Emmenagogues are herbs that stimulate menstruation —which, by the way, is different than inducing miscarriage or abortion.* Emmenagogues are what you use if your period is just being pokey because you're stressed, overworked, underweight, or you have a hormonal or metabolic imbalance.

Parsley

Parsley is a well-known emmenagogue, and is super-nutritious and tasty. Take parsley as an infusion, 2-3 times a day, or eat fresh parsley salads, until your period comes. Other emmenagogues include ginger, yarrow, sage, rosemary, blue cohosh root, and motherwort. You can take these herbs as infusions, 1-3 times a day, for up to a week. Don't use these if you're pregnant.

If your flow is super heavy, try tinctures of yarrow, vitex berry, and red raspberry leaf. Up your intake of iron until you feel better.

* NOTE: I made an executive decision not to cover herbal contraception + abortion in this book — not because I have anything against it, but because I have no experience with it at all. If you need resources on this, check out the amazing women's health zines on page 123.

HEADACHES

Headaches get their own section in this chapter because they are such vicious, elusive little buggers. As anyone who has dealt with chronic headaches knows, painkillers —even herbal ones— are often not enough to solve the problem, because your headache may very well be a mere symptom of a larger problem, like:

- bacterial infection
- allergies
- poor vision
- PMS
- stress
- and more!

But I'm not trying to freak you out. If one of the herbal pain relief tinctures on page 40 doesn't work for you, you're most likely stressed out or dehydrated. If you find yourself in this situation often, try some basic aromatherapy. The essential oils of lavender, peppermint, and chamomile are well-known stress relievers. If you keep a bottle of this blend around, you'll find it useful in all sorts of formulas. Try mixing a few drops with unscented soap or lotion and massage your neck and temples. Or just keep it around and inhale the scent when you're feeling stressed.

You can also use your new blend in an herbal eye pillow. Cut a square of soft fabric into an 8 x 8 swatch and fold it in half with the right sides facing in. Using a tight stitch, sew up one short side and one long side. Turn the pouch inside out.

① ⎡ 8" ⎤ ② ③ TA DA!
  │ ★ ★ ★ │ 8"
  │ ★ ★ │

Meanwhile, mix together ½ - ¾ c rice or flax seeds, ¼ c lavender flowers, and a few drops of essential oil (the lavender/chamomile/mint mix, or whatever you prefer). Pour this stuff into the eye pouch and sew up the remaining side. Lay back and place this pillow over your eyes whenever you're suffering from headaches, insomnia, anxiety, or hangover.

If your headache is accompanied by an uncomfortable smothery feeling, you may have a sinus infection. These are usually treated with antibiotics. Whether or not you decide to take that route, here are some ways to make yourself more comfortable:

• Whenever you can, spend some time under a warm, steamy shower. This loosens mucus and makes blowing your nose easier.

• To make DIY mentholated rub, sans menthol, make a salve with eucalyptus, peppermint, basil, fennel, and some camphor if you can get it. Rub some on your chest and throat before you go to bed to ease congestion as you sleep.

• You can also use those same herbs, in essential oil form, to make bath salts. Add a drop or two of each oil to a cup of sea salt or epsom salts. Stir the salts into a steamy bath. Store in an airtight container if you're not using them right away.

• The best way to fight any sort of infection is to avoid excess stress on body systems, and to try and strengthen your immune system as much as you can. Immunity tonics can include herbs like echinacea, goldenseal, nettles and parsley. The latter two of these are full of vitamins & minerals and make a great tea (or salad) in their own right. Just make sure you cook or crush the stingers out of your nettles!

Echinacea

And now...

Natural Pain Relief! Thank God!

Sometimes you just feel crappy. Your back hurts or your head hurts or your uterus hurts and deep breathing alone is not cutting it. For those special moments, the following herbs can help:

White Willow Bark contains *salicylic acid,* which in 1853 was dismantled by French chemists and synthesized into what we know as aspirin. But folks were using the bark for centuries before that, as a painkiller, fever reducer, and anti-inflam-matory. White willow is best taken as a tea or a tincture, and should not be taken long term, as it can irritate your stomach like aspirin.

* Note: As with aspirin, white willow bark should not be given to young children.

Wild Lettuce is also called opium lettuce - guess why! Wild lettuce is most often used as an analgesic, sleep aid and sedative. Take as a tea or tincture.

Meadowsweet, like willow, contains salicylic acid, and unlike willow, it actually tastes pleasant. Make a tea out of the flowers, or chew a small hunk of peeled root.

Other helpful herbs include red raspberry, slippery elm, and valerian. I'll talk more about these in other sections.

depression and anxiety

And now we come to what will most likely be the most earnest page of this book. Dealing with mental health issues in a holistic way is, I think, incredibly effective and heartening. But for the record, let me state that I am not in any way against using pharmaceuticals to treat depression. I know a lot of people find them creepy, oppressive, and over-prescribed. While I think that some of these criticisms are quite valid, I would also wager that few of the critics themselves have had to live with debilitating depression. My point is this: get help any way you can. If you try herbs and they don't work for your brain, get the help that is right for you. It doesn't make you weak and it doesn't mean you're selling out. Moving on...

St John's Wort is far and away the most popular herb for depression and/or anxiety. The SJW is most effective for mild to moderate depression, so it's perfect for people who want to manage depression but don't feel they need prescription meds. Try taking 15-30 drops of St John's Wort tincture in a cup of warm water, juice or tea 1-3 times each day.

NOTE : This is important! If you take...

......birth control pills.....
......anti-depressants (prescription)......
......anti-coagulant meds (blood thinners).....
......certain HIV/AIDS meds......

...do not take St. John's Wort! Or use a condom! Compounds in SJW decrease the effectiveness of these medications. SJW can also make your skin more sensitive to sunlight, so wear sunscreen if you're taking it on a regular basis.

Other herbs that are good for depression include ginseng, licorice root, lemon balm and chamomile. Ginseng is good for foggy minds and lethargy, and is best used by folks whose depression does not include a lot of anxiety or restlessness. Licorice root is an allover glandular tonic and can help with hypothyroidic depression. Lemon balm and chamomile are both very calm-ing, comforting herbs and are nice to take as a tea even if you're not depressed or anxious.

Licorice Root

Before I end this section I wanted to mention two very effective and famous herbal sedatives: valerian root and kava root. Both of these are excellent soothers in times of stress or trauma.

Valerian is especially useful for insomnia *and menstrual cramps. The root is widely available and it's *seriously effective* - don't drive, bike, or operate a forklift after you take it. Valerian smells quite disgusting, so you will probably want to put your tincture in some juice.

≷FUN FACT≷ Rats, cats and horses also respond to the effects of valerian.

Valerian

* *Kava* is a tropical root native to the Western Pacific. In a lot of cultures, kava holds a cultural importance not unlike that of alcohol or tea in other parts of the world; people drink kava beverages together in order to relax and enjoy each other's company. Kava is great because it relaxes you without sacrificing your mental clarity, so you can actually function. (It also numbs your mouth and throat a tiny bit, just to let you know.) Kava is available via mail order.

NOTE: There's been some controversy as to the effects of kava on the liver. If you are worried about this, practice moderation and do not combine kava with any sort of alcohol. Try a nice kava tea instead.

Kava

chapter 2

Nontoxic
Cleaning
+
Body
Care

Even if you really hate cleaning, I think most people will agree that having a clean and comfortable living space is lovely. Right? However, if TV and print ads are any indication, a lot of us have some seriously messed up ideas about dirt and cleanliness. We seem to think that in order to keep flesh-eating germs from devouring our families we need to bomb our houses and scrub our skins with anti-septic cleansers, the use of which mysteriously correlates with rising rates of chemical sensitivities and antibiotic-resistant supergerms. Plenty of folks are opting for the many "green" products popping up like weeds, but most of this stuff is too expensive to be accessible, or it's made by the same companies that make the mainstream products — so, even though you're trying not to, you're still giving them your money. It makes you wonder, are we really keeping ourselves healthy this way? Why on earth should we spend so much money just to make our lives comfortable?

Fortunately, there is a way to clean your home and your self without donning a fumigation suit: make your own cleaners! It's quite easy, and you'll be taking something practical and imbuing it with your own resourcefulness and creativity. That in itself is quite fulfilling.

Here are some more reasons to make your own cleaners:

• Sometimes germs are dangerous. But you know what's always dangerous? Neurotoxin! Chemicals like chlorine bleach, ammonia, and hydrochloric acid may be effective cleaning agents, but they are harmful to the nervous and respiratory systems, especially over long periods of exposure.

• For the price of a couple bottles of commercial product, you can keep yourself in DIY cleaners and body care for months + months. Plus, every ingredient in this chapter has tons of other uses.

• Homemade products are much gentler to folks who have sensitive skin or chemical sensitivities. They're also safer for kids and animals.

• The recipes in this book employ essential oils, herbs, and herbal infusions for their scents and chemical properties. So if you want your kitchen to smell like a lemon, or a forest, or a lemon forest, *it actually will*!

• Ingredients like castile soap and vinegar are gentle on the earth. Many soaps and detergents and cosmetics are made with byproducts of the oil industry, tested on animals, and then sold in a ridiculous amount of packaging. If you DIY, you can bypass this grossness and make biodegradable, ethical, and responsible products that you'll be proud to use!

basic ingredients
for cleanin'

The following is a list of basic tools and ingredients that you'll need to make the recipes in this chapter. All of them should be available in any, well-stocked grocery store.

- vinegar (use cheap, white distilled vinegar unless specified) - cleanser, deodorizer, grease-cutter
- baking soda - deodorizer, mild abrasive
- ★ borax (aka $Na_2B_4O_7 \cdot 10H_2O$) - natural mineral disinfectant and cleanser
- salt — disinfectant, astringent, abrasive
- lemon juice — grease-cutter, cleanser, deodorizer
- ★ washing soda (aka sodium carbonate) - strips grease and wax, deodorizes
- castile soap - see my love letter on the next page
- essential oils - serve myriad purposes
- dried herbs
- cornstarch - absorbs oil, thickener
- hydrogen peroxide - disinfectant + non-chlorine bleach
- Vitamin C + aspirin - mild acids + exfoliants
- Canola oil - wood conditioner

★ = wear gloves when handling

In addition to these basic ingredients, you'll need some hardware. It's a good idea to take a thrifting trip and get these things even if you already have them, so you'll have some tools exclusively for DIY non-food purposes. If this is out of your budget, clean everything *very* well. Here's what you need:

- ∅ measuring cups and spoons
- ∅ at least one funnel
- ∅ a mixing utensil (use non-reactive metal or plastic)
- ∅ cheesecloth, muslin, or some old nylons - for straining stuff
- ∅ a saucepan w/ a lid - enamel, glass or steel
- ∅ an old blender or egg beater
- ∅ latex gloves (to use when blending ingredients, if you have sensitive skin or are pregnant)
- ∅ a buttload of containers, like:
  - spray bottles
  - squirt bottles
  - jugs
  - plastic tubs
  - squeeze bottles
  - dark glass bottles
  - pickle jars
  - mason jars
  - ...and so on.

Castile

The name "castile soap" originally referred to a type of Spanish soap made from the area's native olive oil. Nowadays the name is given to any soap that is made with vegetable fats (usually hemp, palm, or olive oils) rather than animal fats like tallow. The result is soap in its gentlest, most basic form, which makes it ideal for cleaning pretty much everything. Not only is castile soap extremely versatile, it's cruelty-free, inexpensive, widely available, and in liquid form it's a great base for other herbal ingredients. You can usually find it under a couple different brand names at supermarkets, and in bulk at co-ops + health food stores.

I'm not going to provide a recipe for soap in this book — at least, not from-scratch soap. This chapter is about nontoxic cleaning, and all soaps are made with lye, a caustic alkaline that's about as toxic as you can get. I just didn't feel that it was a fitting recipe for this book. However, making your own soap is super fun and I urge you to take a class or check out a book on the subject, and learn to do it safely.

Soap!

Almost All-Purpose Spray Cleaner

1 t liquid castile soap   1 t borax
2 T white vinegar   2 c hot water
1/4 t each eucalyptus and lavender oil
3 drops tea tree oil

  · Mix all ingredients together in a spray bottle. You can use this on anything besides glass – spray it on, scrub, and rinse off with a clean, damp cloth.

Disinfecting Soft Soap

5 c grated soap (castile)   1/2 c baking soda
6 c hot peppermint or lemon peel tea
1 t eucalyptus essential oil   1 t borax

  · Combine the soap and tea in a 3 quart stainless steel saucepan. Simmer 15 minutes on low heat, stirring occasionally. Add the remaining ingredients, one at a time. Stir well and, using a funnel, pour into a jug or squirt bottle. Shake well before using and apply with a sponge or brush.

Windows

Basic Window Cleaner

3 t liquid soap

3/4 c white vinegar

1/2 t baking soda

4-8 drops lemon oil

Combine all ingredients in a spray bottle. Shake well before using.

Mirror Cleaner

1 1/2 c white vinegar

1/2 c water

4-8 drops orange, lemon, or grapefruit essential oil

Combine all ingredients in a spray bottle. Shake well before using.

For both of these cleaners, just spray on + wipe off. But don't use paper towels! They're wasteful and they suck. Wipe off the cleaner with a soft, lint-free cloth or crumpled newspapers instead.

(...Wood, and Upholstery.)

Wall Cleaner

1 c vinegar
1 gallon water

*use this to shine + remove dust. For grimy walls, use Lemon Floor Cleaner on page 53

• Combine in a bucket & apply with a sponge.

Gentle Wood Cleanser

½ c canola oil
¼ c liquid castile soap
¼ c water

• Combine and shake well before using. Apply with a rag, finish with a dry rag, and follow with polish.

Fabric Cleaner

1 c water
⅛ c liquid castile soap
½ t baking soda
1 T vinegar

• Combine in a spray bottle. Spray onto fabric, scrub with a sponge, and rinse with a little clean water. Blot with a clean rag.

FLOORS

...of all varieties...

• WOOD FLOOR CLEANER •

1½ c water   1½ c vinegar   20 drops peppermint oil

- Combine all ingredients in a spray bottle. Use sparingly, spraying and dry-mopping as you go. Work on small sections of floor at a time. Give it another swipe with a dry mop to make the wood nice and shiny.

• LEMON FLOOR CLEANER •

1 c liquid castile soap
¼ c lemon juice
10 drops tea tree essential oil
6 c warm water

- Mix all ingredients and store in a plastic jug.

• PINE FLOOR CLEANER •

1 c liquid castile
½ c pine oil
6 c warm water

- Mix all ingredients and store in a plastic jug.

for vinyl and tile

• CARPET CLEANER •

3 c water   ¾ c liquid castile   2-3 drops peppermint oil

- Mix all ingredients in a blender, until it is very foamy. Rub the foam into your carpet with a damp sponge, let dry and then vacuum.

• DRY METHOD FOR CARPET •

- Sprinkle the carpet with equal parts baking soda and borax, and then vacuum.

Liquid Dish Soap — not for the dishwasher!

Add up to 30 drops essential oil of your choice to 20 ounces liquid castile soap. I recommend citrus oils or lemon verbena for any sort of kitchen cleaner. If you use a soap that's already scented (like Dr. Bronner's), you can combine scents.

Sink Volcano! Sink Cleanser

¼ c baking soda   ½ c vinegar

Apply to a wet sink, scrub and rinse well.

DIY Drain Opener

Pour 1 c each salt + baking soda, plus ½ c vinegar down the drain. Let it sit for 15 minutes, and then flush the drain with 2 -3 quarts of boiling water.

☆ ✶ Add ½ c vinegar or lemon juice to your dishwater to help cut grease. ✶

toilets & tubs

Soft Scrub

1 c baking soda

1/4 c liquid castile

3-5 drops tea tree oil

2 aspirins, powdered

Mix all ingredients together + add enough water to make a paste. Keep in a shampoo bottle. To use, apply with a sponge, scrub + rinse thoroughly.

Toilet Cleaner

2 c water

1/4 c liquid castile

1 T tea tree oil or grapefruit essential oil

Combine everything in a spray bottle.
Spray on ⇒ wipe off!

Bowl Cleaner - with SCIENCE!

1/2 c baking soda

1/4 c vinegar

10 drops tea tree oil

★ To deodorize curiously gross-smelling drains, sprinkle a handful of baking soda down the drain when it's dry ★

Combine everything, pour into the toilet + scrub away.
Note: since this stuff explodes a little, each recipe = 1 cleaning.

Laundry

All-Purpose Laundry Soap

This is a low-lathering, unscented detergent you can use in a washing machine. If you want to scent it, you can dry and pulverize some scented castile soap (like Dr. Bronner's) to use in the recipe, or add a few drops of your favorite essential oil.

This recipe makes enough for three loads, but is very easily doubled or tripled.

½ cup baking soda

½ cup powdered castile soap

¼ cup washing soda

¼ cup borax

* NOTE: In order for the soap powder to dissolve, use warm or hot water in your machine. o

Mix ingredients well, add essential oils if you're using them, and stir again to break up any clumps. Use ½ cup per load.

Fabric Softener Pouch

Technically this is a sachet — but I don't like the word "sachet." I like the word "**pouch**." First, make a pouch out of tightly woven fabric by folding a rectangle of cloth in half and sewing up the sides: ① ② BAM!
Make a couple of these and fill each with a couple spoonfuls of this mixture:

½ c baking soda

1 T arrowroot powder

1 T rice flour or cornstarch

1-3 drops essential oil (your choice)

Tie up the pouch tightly and pop it in the dryer with your clothes. Make a couple with different scents — lavender is nice for bedsheets and lemon verbena for clothing. Refill the pouch when the scent fades.

＊A *sportive alternative:* let a couple of (clean) tennis balls bounce around with your laundry, to create air pockets and hence, fluffy freshness.

Homemade Bleach

1 c hydrogen peroxide
3 T lemon juice
15 c water

Mix all ingredients together + keep in a large plastic bottle.

Spray Starch

3 T plus 1 t cornstarch
4 cups warm water

Mix really well so no lumps remain, and keep in a spray bottle.

Tips!

If you have a piece of clothing that bleeds or dyes your skin, try handwashing it with a few glugs of vinegar in the washwater.

Dry cleaning is kind of a scam. For most clothes that "require" dry cleaning, gentle hand-washing will suffice. Use All Purpose Laundry Soap or baby shampoo and dry it flat on a clean towel. Wool fibers like acid, so if you're washing wool, use castile and add vinegar to the soapy water.

Stain Removers

*rub on your chosen antidote + launder as usual

★ Washing Soda is one of the best stain removers around. Make a paste with a little water and use it on:

- wine
- berries
- grease stains
- blood and other proteins
- coffee
- tea
- most other food stains
- sweat
- urine

★ Borax, like washing soda, is alkaline and thus dissolves acidic and protein-based stains, like the ones above. It also works really well on mildew. If you have hard water, use borax instead of washing soda, which will leave a chalky residue on fabric.

★ Vegetable oil is good for removing gummy labels and stickers.

★ Vinegar is acidic and removes alkalines like:

- grass
- rust
- paint
- ink

★ If you can't treat a stain right away, at least give it a rinse. Use only cold water, especially with proteins like blood. Heat will only cook the proteins and set the stain. Ew.

★ Glycerin is very sticky and slippery and is best used on oily or waxy stains, like lipstick.

★ Club soda will remove most of the stains listed under "washing soda." You can spray it on, dampen a towel with it, or just pour it on. It's a real amiable little product.

★ Once and for all: gum needs to be frozen and then pulled or chipped off. Smearing more crap on it does not work. Ok!

pest control

The key to keeping mice + bugs out of your space is to understand how they get in and why they want to be there. Once you know that, a bit of prevention and - sorry - scrupulous cleaning will keep them from hanging around.

- Your house is full of free food, so cover up your leftovers (and your kitchen's compost bin), wipe your counters, and take your trash + recycling out often. Don't leave food lying around, especially at night. The cleaner your place is, the less likely bugs are to inhabit it.

- Consider calling a truce with non-poisonous house spiders. They eat lots of flying insects, and contrary to popular belief, they hardly ever bite people.

- Keep potted plants or bundles of dried herbs around your kitchen, or wherever you're having an infestation. I keep most of my herbs in my kitchen and they've done a rad job of protecting my food against fruit flies. Bugs and mice especially hate: peppermint, oregano, basil, garlic, rosemary, lavender, lemon balm, hot peppers, and citrus peels.

- For nasty fruit fly infestations, make a trap: pour ½ inch of old wine in a jar, cover the mouth of the jar with plastic, and poke a few holes in the top. The flies'll be able to get in, and get drunk, but they won't come out.

Pest Repellant Powder

For flies, ticks, fleas, mosquitoes, roaches, ants, and mice — this just repels pests, it doesn't kill them.

2 handfuls dried peppermint

A healthy pinch each: garlic powder, cayenne, lavender flowers, lemon peel, and dried basil

Grind everything very finely and store in an airtight container. You can mix the herbs with some salt, if you like. Sprinkle the powder any place bugs like to hang out: in back of your cupboards, under your fridge/oven, around windows + doors, along baseboards, etc.

BIG GUNS! (If you need them)

· Borax is effective for killing bugs. Mix some with sugar and sprinkle it across doorways and along baseboards. Do not use this if you have kids or pets.

· You can spray lines of ants with diluted peppermint castile soap. The soap will kill the ants and erase the pheromone trail so other ants won't be able to follow.

· Make fly traps by painting strips of heavy paper with corn syrup or honey. Let it dry until it's tacky and then hang them up.

Random Messes
and how to destroy them

Lemon Rub for Copper + Brass

· Dip half a fresh lemon in salt and rub it over tarnished metal. Wash with soapy water, rinse and buff dry.

Oven Cleaner

· Scrub a *cold* oven with equal parts vinegar + water. If something spills in your oven, pour salt on the spill while the oven is still warm, and sweep out the salt with a brush when everything's cool.

Killing the Fridge Demon

· Clean your refrigerator's walls, shelves and drawers with a solution of ½ c water, 3 T baking soda, and 6 drops essential oil of your choice.

· To absorb weird smells, leave a small, open box of baking soda in a corner of the fridge. Alternately, you can use a small bowl of coffee grounds (unused coffee grounds, thanks). These two tricks work well for musty freezers, also.

baking soda battles the fearsome fridge demon

Gross Food Tips

· If your cooking pot is crusty with burnt stuff, scrub it with baking soda while it's still hot. Method 2: Use the pot to boil some water with a couple spoonfuls of baking soda thrown in. Let it sit until the food can be scraped off.

· For really greasy dishes, add ½ c lemon juice or vinegar to your dishwater.

Appliance Cleaner

· Mix together 2 parts each vinegar + lemon juice and 1 part water. Let sit on stains and scrub with a sponge. Don't leave your appliances plugged in when you clean them!

Cleaning a Coffeemaker

· Fill the coffee maker's water resevoir ¼ full with white vinegar, and add water until totally full. Turn the little guy on and let the cleaner drip into the pot. Turn the maker off and let it cool. Pour the vinegar-water solution back into the resevoir and let it cycle through again. Repeat once more. Pour out the vinegar solution and replace with clean water. Let that cycle through twice, and then wash both the coffee pot and the grounds basket in warm, soapy water.

oh, thank you!

Choosing Herbs for Your Skin & Hair ⭐

Here's a convenient table for when you're choosing oils or herbs to add to your formulations. Notice that rose, lavender, and licorice are excellent choices in any situation.

Herb/Oil	oily	dry	sensi-tive	Anti-bacterial
Aloe Vera		★		
Birch				★
Calendula		★	★	
Chamomile		★	★	
Cinnamon				★
Comfrey		★	★	
Eucalyptus				★
Horsetail	★	★		
Lavender	★	★	★	★
Lemon Balm	★			
Lemon Verbena	★			
Lemongrass				★
Licorice	★	★	★	
Mint	★	★		
Nettle		★		
Orange Blossom		★		
Rose	★	★	★	★
Rosemary	★			★
Sage	★			
St. John's Wort		★		
Sweet Orange				★
Tea Tree	★			★
Thyme				★
Witch Hazel	★			

Remember that bottle of castile soap you used to clean your whole living space? Pour some on your head! Castile soap is so basic that it can clean pretty much any part of you besides your eyeballs. To make a gentle soap for your hair and skin, mix 12 oz. of unscented castile soap with up to 30 drops of an essential oil or oils suitable for your hair and skin type. Cap the bottle, give it a shake, and that's it!

... Except, not really. You see, regular shampoos do not contain soap, they contain detergents like the dreaded ☠ sodium laureth sulfate ☠, or SLS. For a while people thought SLS caused cancer. For the most part that idea has been debunked, but it is still true that SLS is rather irritating to skin.

Detergents like SLS are cheap, very foamy, and very effective, because they strip oil and dirt from surfaces (your dishes, your clothes, or your face) and then rinse clean. Castile soap, on the other hand, does not strip oils quite as well, and is much gentler on your skin. The downside to all this loving gentleness is that castile can leave a bit of residue on your hair.

A lot of folks don't mind this, or even prefer it, but if you want that squeaky-clean feeling, you'll have to cut the residue with a mild acid. Try rinsing your hair with a coffeemug-full of diluted lemon juice or vinegar after you shampoo. Make sure to rinse again with clean water if you don't want to smell like a gherkin.

Soapwort Shampoo

Soapwort is a funny little shrub that contains natural saponins (soap-like chemicals) which cause the flesh of the plant to lather when agitated. A decoction of soapwort root (or its tropical neighbor, soap bark) can be used as a gentle cleanser for hair and skin. The nettles in this recipe add shine + body to hair, and the lemon verbena smells nice.

*NOTE: this will not be as foamy as regular shampoo, so don't worry if you can't work up a huge lather with this stuff.

2 c distilled water
1½ T dried, chopped soapwort root
1 t dried (2 t fresh) lemon verbena
1 t dried nettles
Optional: a couple drops of essential oil suitable for your hair type

1. Get yourself a big jar with a lid, put the soapwort root and water inside, and let it soak overnight. ⓓ

2. In the morning, pour the whole mess into a saucepan and bring it to a boil. Reduce the heat to low, cover, and let simmer for 20 minutes. ⓓ

3. Remove the pan from the heat and add nettles and lemon verbena. Mix well and allow to cool completely. ⓓ

ⓓ 4. Line a funnel with cheesecloth (several layers), muslin, or the foot from an old pair of nylons. Place the spout of the funnel in a squirt or pump bottle and decant your new shampoo. Squeeze the solids to get out the last bit of liquid before tossing. ⓓ ⓓ

5. If you're using essential oils, add them now. Cap the bottle and give it a good shake. ⓓ

ⓓ ★ This shampoo keeps for up to 10 days on the shelf, a day or two longer in the fridge. You can take advantage of this and make a really nice shampoo to use in the summer. Replace the nettles in the recipe with some nice invigorating rosemary, and add a couple drops of tea tree or peppermint essential oil at the end. Keep it in the fridge and use it any time you need a cheap (and homemade!) thrill.

Baking Soda Shampoo

I don't think this even counts as a recipe. Basically: try using baking soda instead of shampoo. Just rub a couple teaspoons of baking soda into the roots of your hair while it's wet, and rinse off in the shower. The soda will clean your hair and dissolve any product build-up. If you really like using liquid shampoo, you might also try mixing a teaspoon each of baking soda and shampoo and using that to wash your hair. The combination of the two is awesome for dissolving serious product build-up.

Homemade Conditioners
→ aka *Godsend* or *Greasehead?*

I have tried many homemade conditioners in my time, including olive oil, egg yolks, mayo, mashed bananas, and avocado. And I <u>always</u> end up with stubborn chunks of fruit, cooked eggs, or ungodly amounts of grease in my hair. I'm not saying that egg yolks don't work, just that I personally always screw them up; because of this, I don't really feel comfortable suggesting that you put that stuff on your head. What I am going to suggest is that you may not need a conditioner... *at all*! Scandal!

But think about it: commercial shampoos are designed to strip the scalp of the oil it naturally produces, and conditioners are supposed to replace those oils with fruity, pearly goodness. But if you switch your shampoo with a head soap that doesn't strip those oils, why would you need all that extra moisturizer on your head? Makes sense, right? Of course, if you have coarse, thick or dry hair, or you wash your hair often, you'll probably want a conditioner at least some of the time. And here comes one right now!

Vinegar Rinse + Conditioner

4 c very hot water
3/4 c vinegar (cider is nice)
2 T each dried nettles, dried rosemary, and dried chamomile flowers

• Tie the herbs up in a bit of muslin and combine with the other ingredients in a jar. Cover + let steep overnight. In the morning, remove the herb bag. To use, work in up to a cup of the vinegar after you shampoo, and rinse well.

Facial Cleansers

Homemade face soaps are wonderful not only because making and using them is so satisfying, but because they cost a fraction of the price of drugstore cleansers. You can make a big batch of simple cleanser and add different ingredients according to your changing skin, the seasons, your mood, anything!

Simple Face Soap

1 oz grated bar soap - homemade, castile, or your favorite purchased soap, or liquid soap

2 c hot herbal infusion, made with herbs suitable for your skin type, or plain water

Combine soap + water in a jar + let sit overnight so the soap can dissolve. To use, massage a bit into your skin and rinse with water. If you want a foamier cleanser, increase the amount of soap. Other ways to customize:

· add up to five drops of suitable essential oil.

· add witch hazel extract for oily skin, glycerin or honey for dry skin

· add baking soda to make a paste-y, scrubby cleanser

· crush two aspirins into powder and add to the soap to make a cleanser for pimply skin.

· increase the amount of soap in the recipe and use antiseptic herbs and oils to make an antibacterial wash for hands and minor injuries.

Creamy Lavender Cleanser

1 part each: jojoba oil
glycerin (found at drugstores)
cornstarch

3 drops lavender oil

Combine ingredients in a bowl and mix until smooth + creamy. Transfer to a small jar. To use, rub some into your skin, wipe it off with a soft cloth, and rinse well. This cream is like a nice, light cold cream. Since it contains no beeswax or lanolin, it's easy to rinse off and is naturally vegan - just make sure your glycerin is vegetable - derived.

* Rose & Honey Face Wash *

½ c rose water; homemade is best
2 T liquid castile soap
1 t honey
up to 5 drops rose essential oil (optional)

This is easiest if the rose infusion is still warm. Combine the rose water and honey and stir until the honey is dissolved. Add the soap and oils and mix well. Store in a pump bottle and use by rubbing the liquid over your skin and rinse with warm water. This recipe can also be added to your bathwater.

herbal toners ...in your face!

Herbal infusions are really terrific for treating conditions like acne, rosacea, dryness, and so on. If your skin is troubling you, splash or rub some herb-infused water, vinegar, or diluted tincture on your skin after you wash it. Here are some suggested combinations:

• ACNE: peppermint + birch bark-infused vinegars with a few drops of lavender oil

• ALSO ACNE: witch hazel extract infused with sage and lemon balm, plus 10 drops tea tree oil (per cup of infusion)

• ECZEMA: strong infusion of equal parts chamomile, nettles, and calendula, with about a spoonful of Epsom salts dissolved in it

• DRY SKIN: rose-infused water with a spoonful of honey and a few finely-ground almonds

• IRRITATED SKIN: equal parts water and aloe vera juice. Infuse the water with comfrey and calendula.

• ROSACEA: water or vinegar infused with oatmeal (wrap some in a bag, like you're making tea), chamomile and licorice.

• ROUGH SKIN: vinegar infused with birch bark, rose, and chamomile flowers. You can also replace the birch bark with one or two crushed aspirin tablets.

Exfoliation and Other Pleasures

There are basically two ways to exfoliate your skin.*Mechanical scrubs* rely on small particles, like sand, salt, and ground-up plant parts, to create friction that rubs off dead skin cells. Loofahs and brushes work in the same way. Abrasives also increase blood flow to the skin. Even if you don't care about stuff like exfoliation, I heartily recommend giving yourself a good scrub now and then. I use a stiff-bristled brush on my skin every morning before I shower and it makes a huge difference in how awake I feel.

Chemical scrubs, even hundred-dollar schmancy ones, generally depend on hydroxy acids, which work by dissolving the intercellular glue between bits of dead skin. Hydroxy acids are present in many fruits, milk, sugar and other plants like birch. They're seriously everywhere; it's pretty ridiculous that people pay so much money to get them in a jar.

Some notes:

- If you have sensitive skin, avoid really grainy scrubs.
- Scrubs + brushes/loofahs work best on dry skin.
- If you're scrubbing your whole body, do your legs first, then your arms, then your torso. Always rub towards your heart, and be gentle with the skin atop your vital organs.

Scrubby Scrubs

The instructions for all of these are the same: just rub the scrub around on your skin for about 20 seconds (or whatever), and rinse well. Most can be used for face and body; the exceptions would be very coarse, salt-based scrubs, which you should keep to below the neck.

★ for oily skin ★
- baking soda, a crushed aspirin, and enough water to make a paste
- handful of seasalt + 1 T ground sage, moistened with birch or lavender infusion
- sugar moistened with lemon juice
- still-damp coffee grounds (used)
- equal parts milk powder and honey, plus a little lemon juice and cornmeal
- sea salt with 2 drops teatree oil

★ for normal skin ★
- equal parts ground oatmeal and plain yogurt
- a handful of cornmeal moistened with honey
- a slushee of sugar and almond oil or aloe vera gel
- ground dried adzuki beans and a pinch of dried calendula petals, + a little water
- rice flour, a tiny bit of liquid soap, and water
- one or two ground aspirins and a dab of honey
- brown sugar a pinch of ground rose petals, and a wee bit of apple cider vinegar
- sea salt, zest from one lemon, and almond oil

★ for dry skin ★
- equal parts honey and finely-ground almonds
- sea salt + a few drops essential oil + enough olive oil to make a thick slush
- ½ an avocado with enough oat flour to make a paste
- ground flax seeds and a little rose water
- 2 T each ground oats and almonds + 1 T rose water + 1 T heavy cream
- equal parts plain yogurt and ground almonds
- a little plain yogurt mixed with the contents of 1 bag of green tea (about 1 tablespoon).

super precious face oil

This is the stuff I use on my face every day. I love using it: the bergamot, lavender, and clary sage oils make me feel happy and relaxed, and using a dropper makes me feel like a scientist. If you keep this oil in dark glass and away from heat and light, it will last you a very long time.

- 2 oz carrier oil (see below)
- 15 drops essential oil(s) suitable for your skin

For oily skin, use grapeseed oil, hazelnut, or jojoba oils

For normal skin, use almond, jojoba, or apricot kernel oil

For dry skin, use olive, coconut, or macademia nut oil. For really dry skin, mix in some avocado oil also.

Combine the ingredients in a small bowl and funnel it all into a dark glass bottle with a dropper. To use, combine 2-3 drops of oil with 4 drops of warm water. Rub your hands together to emulsify the oil, and pat it on your face until it's absorbed. You can change the ratio of oil to water depending on how dry your skin is.

Some suggestions for essential oils:

- Oily skin: 5 drops each rosemary, clary sage, and bergamot oils
- Normal skin: 5 drops each rose, lavender, and peppermint oil
- Dry skin: 5 drops each chamomile, rose, and orange blossom oil

Easy Deodorant Powder

• Combine equal parts cornstarch and baking soda and add a few drops of an antibacterial essential oil like lavender or tea tree. Store in an airtight jar to preserve the scent. You can slap this on wherever you like — put it on with a powder puff, if you're fancy.

* reduce the amount of baking soda in this recipe to make body powder, which absorbs moisture + prevents chafing

DIY Toothpaste

2 oz chalk (calcium carbonate — found @ hardware stores and online)
1 oz baking soda
Pinch stevia powder (for sweetness)
Vegetable glycerin
5-6 drops peppermint oil

• Combine dry ingredients and oils with enough glycerin to make a paste. Keep the paste in an airtight jar, along with a little spoon to get the paste onto your brush.

• Other good oils include cinnamon, rose, clove, and lemon

• Yes, just plain baking soda (or soda + stevia + peppermint oil) is an easy and effective alternative to this recipe.

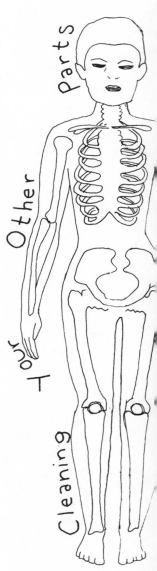

Parts

Other

Your

Cleaning

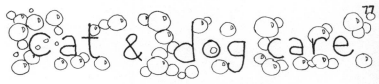

Cat & Dog Care

Basic Dog (and cat) Shampoo

1½ T castile soap - use lightly scented or
  unscented soap
1½ c warm water

Combine soap + water in a jar + shake
to combine. Dampen your dog's fur, rub in
the shampoo, and rinse thoroughly. Make sure
not to get this in your dog's eyes - use a soapy
washcloth to clean his/her face.

If this soap leaves a residue on your dog's
fur, rinse with a cup of vinegar diluted in water.

Fancy: replace the warm water with an
infusion of half lavender and half rose geranium.
This will help repel fleas and ticks.

Dry Shampoo for Cats...and people!

½ c cornstarch
2 T lavender flowers, ground fine

Sprinkle some of this on your cat's fur,
rub it in, and brush out after an hour or so.

★ NOTE: Avoid using essential oils on animals.
If you really feel you need to use them,
make sure they're heavily diluted -
no more than 1 drop
oil to 1 cup
of carrier.

chapter 3

Gardening

Other than killing stuff, making tools, and breeding more of ourselves, gardening is our most enduring hobby as a species. No wonder, then that it can get so incredibly complicated! In researching this chapter, I encountered more techniques, tips, and fussy projects than I thought possible for a process that Nature seems so capable of handling by herself. Human ingenuity, man. And while I think all that stuff is incredible, this chapter will be a very simple affair about growing vegetables. Make that: growing vegetables cheaply and organically. Because what's more DIY than that? It's the greatest nesting skill on Earth! Or at least, it's something that's always interested me, and if you're reading this, it probably interests you too. Ok? Ok!

* Super shoutout: this chapter depended heavily on the superb expertise of my dear friend Ivy Fox, who is a phenomenal gardener and an even better friend. Thanks girl! *

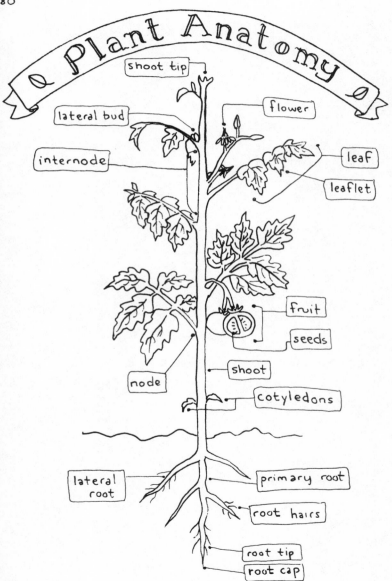

Plant Anatomy

shoot tip

flower

lateral bud

internode

leaf

leaflet

fruit

seeds

shoot

node

cotyledons

lateral root

primary root

root hairs

root tip

root cap

A (very) Brief Glossary* of Gardening Terms

* *

•**Annual**: a plant that completes its life cycle within one year. The life cycle being:

seed → plant → flower → fruit → dead → seed

This means you'll have to plant these every year. It also means that if you don't like something, it's not going to stick around forever. Most vegetables are annuals, and are separated by season and hardiness (frost tolerance). Examples:

•**Perennial:** a plant that dies down to the ground in winter but keeps its roots alive underground, allowing it to grow back in the spring. There are only a few perennial vegetables (rhubarb, asparagus, artichokes) but many perennial herbs, including:

- lavender, thyme, chives, oregano, sage, mint, lemon balm, rosemary, tarragon

Perennials can tolerate a lot more and are generally less wussy than annuals, so consider making a permanent place in your life for them. They also make excellent houseplants!

- **NPK**: if you're shopping for fertilizer you'll see this acronym alot. NPK stands for nitrogen (N), phosphate (P), and potash or potassium (K), which are the three main nutrients plants need. On the fertilizer package you'll also see a number like 10-10-10 or 5-10-5. This refers to the proportion of each nutrient in the fertilizer mix.

- **Mulch**: a material spread over soil in order to maintain the soil's integrity. Mulch helps keep in moisture, maintain a steady temperature, and it keeps weeds from germinating; basically, it's a blanket for your garden. If you want to mulch, make sure you do it when your garden soil is just how you like it – if you mulch overly damp, cold soil, it will stay that way. Some materials that make good mulch: straw, compost, grass clippings, shredded newspaper, gravel, wood chips, and pine needles.

- **Aeration**: the process of loosening soil by digging or tilling. Aerating your soil decompacts dirt and allows air to pass through soil particles.

- **Cultivar**: this term refers to a variety of plant originated by gardeners instead of in the wild.

- **Heirloom**: the definition of an heirloom is hotly debated, but generally, an heirloom is a very old (like, at least 50 years old) cultivar that is not a hybrid.

Assessing your Space

Regardless of whether you are planning to garden in your backyard, your windowsill, or a vacant lot, the first thing you need to do is to take a census of your space and its resources. Here's a list of questions to ask yourself when you're looking around:

Space

• How big is your proposed garden or container? Do you have enough room for a mature root structure? If you want to grow tall plants, do you have the required vertical space?

Sunlight

• When will your garden get direct sunlight? Are there any pesky shade trees or tall buildings nearby? How many sunny days do you get during the warm season?

Water

• Is there a hose or other water source nearby? Is your local climate rainy or arid? How much time are you willing to spend watering? Do you plan to use greywater in your garden?

Soil

• Do you know what kind of soil is prevalent in your area? What other plants are growing in your neighborhood? If you wet down your lawn, how quickly does it dry out again?

84

Weather & Climate ...& Landscape

• Is your area prone to drought, tornadoes, heavy rains or other ill weather? If so, how protected is your garden? Do you live in a city? Do you have to worry about pipes/neighbors/car exhaust? Does your area have any invasive species that should be avoided (like English Ivy in the Northwest U.S.)?

Pests

• Do you know what creatures are waiting to eat your plants? Is your area rural enough to be home to larger herbivores, like rabbits or deer? And what about plant diseases? Are there any that your region is particularly vulnerable to?

I know this self-quiz seems really long, but don't fret - these questions are really just a way for you to remember all the little specifics which seem obvious in retrospect ("I planted roses in the desert and I'm sick of watering them!") but are easy to forget. Doing as much trouble-shooting as you can before you plant will save you a lot of grief later on. If that makes your brain hurt, here are good rules of thumb:
• grow your vegetables on level ground, or in rows cutting across the slope of the ground, to prevent soil erosion.
• make sure your plots are near a water source; use greywater only on non-edibles.

• Vegetables and other edibles will grow best if they get at least 8 hours of sunlight each day, so choose a spot that's not shaded over by trees, buildings, or other structures.

When to plant

Unfortunately, if you're growing stuff outside, you can't really just stick a few seeds in the ground in January and wait for a zucchini to pop out. Different plants have different seasons based on their ability to handle low temperatures, frost, and so on. If you know when to plant each veggie you'll be able to maximize the plant's yield and eat much better. I wish I could draw a little chart and just tell you when to plant what, but alas, I don't know where you live. So you'll need to do two things:

1. If you live in the US, figure out which USDA zone you live in. The USDA splits the nation into 11 "hardiness zones" based on average minimum temperatures. It's kind of an old system, since it was introduced before most people gave a crap about factors like pollution. But gardeners and farmers still use it. You can

find this map in almost any gardening book or
website, and on the USDA's website (which also
has lots of information about specific crops,
invasive species, and, uh, corn prices).

The map is swirly and colorful and would
make a really rad poster. Once you
know your zone, you can look up a
planting schedule, which will tell you
stuff like:

· a plant's frost tolerance and the
length of its season;

· minimum soil and air temperatures
for many different vegetables; and

· the best times of year to start
seeds (more on that later) and to plant
them in the ground.

You can look up planting schedules
online or in a farmer's almanac. If
you live outside the US, check your
government's agricultural agency for
information on planting.

A lot of gardeners like to apply a
more intuitive approach to timing,
because it fosters a deeper connection
between them and the earth. I think
that's really lovely; but I also
think that beginning food-growers
should try planting by the books
for a year or two and then
work from there.

Making Beds

If you only do two things to your garden, let them be these: ① work some compost into your soil, and ② build a raised and/or sunken bed. Why? Because I like watching you sweat! Just kidding. Because adjusting the height of your garden can solve a lot of problems. A raised bed will increase drainage, reduce the number of weeds, snails and slugs amongst your veggies, and will make gardening more accessible to folks with limited mobility. A sunken bed will help sandy or otherwise dry soil retain moisture + nutrients. Whichever style you choose, you will need some rot-resistant wood (like red cedar) if you can get it. You can certainly use any untreated lumber you like, but tough woods like cedar will make for long-lasting beds. Depending on how high you want your bed to be, you can use one plank per side, or stack them. Length and width are also up to you, but keep in mind that if you can't reach the middle of the bed you're going to feel silly. 6' x 4' is a good bed size, and you can certainly make more than one per yard. If all types of wood are beyond your budget, cement blocks are an easy, scavenge-able alternative, as are bricks and stones joined with or without mortar.

① Plot the size and shape of your bed by pounding in some wooden stakes at the corners of the planned bed. String rope or twine between the stakes.

② Inside this shape, dig up as much vegetation as you can. If you're not planning to plant for a few months, you can cover the ground with plastic to kill off any weeds. Leave the plastic on for 2 months or so. Once you have a bare patch of earth, work it well with a shovel.

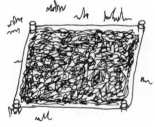

③ Place your planks with their long ends against the stakes. Get a friend to help you hold the planks while you check the tops of the planks with a level (if you care). Secure the planks to the stakes with wood screws. If you like, you can tack on some metal brackets outside

the frame using wood screws or nails.

④ If you're making a very tall bed, keep stacking + securing planks atop the first until the bed is as high as you'd like it to be.

⑤ Time to fill your bed! You can use soil from other parts of your yard, potting mix, layers of dirt and compost and mulch - whatever you like!

If you want to build a sunken bed, the process is similar. Basically, you'll need to dig out a very large, shallow hole, place the stake-and-plank frame inside it, and tamp the dirt down around the outside of the frame.

⭑ A pretty awesome amendment to a raised bed: a tiny greenhouse! Collect a couple of hula hoops of equal diameter, saw each in half, tape or otherwise secure their feet to a couple of 2×4"s (as shown), and cover the whole thing with plastic! RAD.

×2   ← tarp =

tips for garden layout

Make sure beds are at least a foot and a half apart from each other, so you have someplace to walk. Planks or flat rocks will keep it dry.

• Plant as far as you can away from trees and shrubs. Not only will they shade your garden, their roots will suck up water + nutrients.

• Keep annuals and perennials in separate beds or in separate areas of the garden. Woody herbs, for example, need less water than many annuals, and in the fall, you'll be able to clean up your annual beds without disturbing the still-living perennials.

• Plant your tallest veggies (corn, trellised vines, etc.) at the north end of your garden, and your low-growers at the south end. This way all your plants get that lovely southern sun.

• Save very sunny spots for fruit-bearing plants and roots. A good rule is that if a plant is made up mostly of green leaf, it can tolerate more shade than one that isn't. Lettuces, collards, cabbages and so on grow well in partial shade because the large surface area of their leaves makes for maximum sunlight absorbtion.

• Try your hand at companion planting: plant rows of early bloomers like salad greens and radishes in between rows of long-term crops like peppers. You'll save a ton of space this way, because you'll harvest those short-term veggies before the peppers are big enough to need that extra room.

• If your goal is to actually subsist mainly on your garden, plant several varieties of a vegetable you eat a lot, like an onion or carrot. The different plants will take varying lengths of time to mature, so you'll have a steady income of onions over a couple months instead of a buttload of them in the same week.

• Annual veggies are basically divided into cool season crops and warm season crops. You can start early in the year and plant a quick-growing crop, harvest in the spring and immediately replace it with a summer crop. Repeat in the fall with some hardy broccoli or root veggies, and you'll get three harvests out of one patch of dirt. CHA-CHING!

• Herbs are awesome to have in your garden, but certain types can get way out of control. Mint and yarrow are notorious for this. Consider keeping a separate bed for herbs, or even better, plant herbs in containers, inside or outside your home.

The Buddy System

Plants are sort of like superheroes: each has its own specialty (bug-repelling, nitrogen-fixing, etc.), but when you let them hang out together, those advantages are compounded. Try using plant buddies if you find yourself using a lot of fertilizer or bug spray.

Plant	Good Buddies	Bad Buddy
Beans	carrots, corn, radishes, peas, lettuce	onions
Beets	beans (bush), cabbage, onions	
Cabbage	beets, celery, onions, tomatoes	strawberry
Carrots	beans, lettuce, peas, radishes, tomatoes	
Corn	beans, squash, melons, peas	
Cucumber	beans, corn, lettuce, onions, radishes	strong herbs
Lettuce	carrots, cukes, radish, strawberries	
Melons	corn, radishes	
Onions	beets, carrots, celery, cucumber, peppers, tomatoes, squash	beans, peas
Peas	beans, carrots, radishes, turnips	onions
Peppers	onions	
Radishes	beans, carrots, melons, lettuce	
Spinach	celery, eggplant, cauliflower	
Squash	corn, onion, radishes	
Strong Herbs	cabbage, peppers, tomatoes	cucumber
Strawberry	beans, lettuce, onion, spinach	cabbage
Tomatoes	cabbage, carrots, spinach	corn
Zucchini	corn, onions, radishes	

dirt aint dirt: testing and improving your soil

There are several soil-based factors that influence which plants will grow where. The first of these is soil texture or composition. Besides bugs, rocks and roots, soil is generally made up of clay, silt, and sand. If you have very sandy or clayey soil, it's going to change what kind of care you give your plants and what will grow well there. Here are two ways to test your soil's texture:

Method 1: Dirt Ballin'

· Grab a handful of recently-watered soil and roll it into a little ball. If it holds tightly and is tacky to the touch, you have clay soil. If it will not stick together and is sharp or gritty-feeling, it's sandy soil. If it holds somewhat and feels soft, like a river bed, it's mostly silt.

Method 2: Dirt Parfait!

· Fill a large jar 2/3 full with water. Add a squirt of dish soap and fill the jar the rest of the way with dirt. Shake well and let settle for 2 days. The dirt will separate into three layers as shown at left. Naturally, the biggest layer is what your soil is mostly made of.

If what you see in your jar has about equal parts sand and silt, with slightly less clay, congratulations! This means you've got loam soil, which is very nice soil indeed: it drains well and also retains needed moisture and nutrients. Don't freak if you don't have loam soil! You can still have a rad garden — you just need to either adjust your soil or reconsider what plants you want to grow. To adjust very clayey or sandy soils, work compost into the first foot or so of soil. If your beds are still too moist, consider building raised beds to increase drainage. If your soil needs constant watering, a sunken bed can help.

An alternative to all of this is to simply sow plants that like to live in the type of soil you have. This might narrow your choices a bit, but it's a very sustainable way to garden. For sandy soil, try planting:

- root vegetables, vines and leafy veggies, like:
  - tomatoes
  - squashes
  - potatoes
  - carrots
  - spinach
  - peppers
  - strawberries
  - corn
  - lettuces

★ keep in mind that sand drains quickly and if you don't build a sunken bed, you'll have to water often.

★ nutrients leach quickly in sandy soil, so you might need to fertilize more often

For heavy clay and silt soils, plant these:

> • shallow rooted plants, like pear trees
> • virtually all members of the large + tasty Brassicaceae family:
>   • broccoli
>   • cauliflower
>   • cabbages
>   • kohlrabi
>   • kale
>   • Brussels sprouts

• clay soil is fertile and nutrient-rich, but does not drain well. If you don't build a raised bed, work your soil well to decompact it, and cut down on your watering.

Once you've worked out your soil texture, you need to determine its pH. On the standard pH scale, ideal soil is about here:

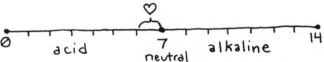

To test your pH, get a kit from a garden store, or send a jar of dirt to your local county extension office for testing (www.csrees.usda.gov/Extension).

• Very alkaline soil can be corrected by working in sawdust, wood chips, or partially rotted leaves.

• Very acidic soil can be corrected by adding crushed oyster shells or wood ashes.

• An inch of compost worked into the soil will balance slightly acidic or alkaline soil. It will also improve drainage, fertility, and everything else!

Compost for beginners

Everyone loves composting. It's a fact! Tending a compost heap is the easiest, cheapest, most environmentally sound way to create healthy soil for your garden. If you don't already have a compost pile in your yard or apartment complex, here's how it should go down:

① Grab a trash bag and a bucket. Use the bag(s) to collect stuff like paper scraps, straw, dead leaves, and other dry material. What you'll have is a bag full of carbon-rich substance that will form the base of your compost.

Meanwhile, fill the bucket with nitrogen-rich matter like grass clippings, food scraps, aged manure (see note), and so on. Many of my friends keep a lil' bucket under their sink just for compost fodder. FYI, you can also compost:

- bread products
- egg- and nutshells
- flat beer
- lint
- wood ashes
- junk mail (shredded)

② Find a spot in your yard and, if you wish, build an enclosure for your compost. You could buy one, of course, but it's just as easy to nail some pallets together, or bend some wire mesh into a cylinder. A big pile in a corner of the yard is also fine.

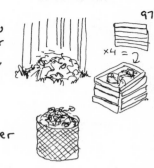

③ To build your compost, start with a bed of dry, carbon-y stuff about 6 inches deep. On top of that, spread a 2 inch deep layer of nitrogen material. Then, the icing, as it were: a shovelfull of dirt from your garden. The garden soil will introduce the organisms that will be making your compost.

④ Repeat these three layers until the pile is about three feet tall. This part goes by very quickly if you have some friends and a couple of extra shovels. Try to keep the ratio of dry stuff to moist stuff at around 3:1.

⑤ Water your compost until the whole thing is just damp, but not wet.

whee!

⑥ Over the next couple of months, this pile should get quite warm. This is a good sign, as it signals that decomposition is taking place. If, after a month, it's not warm at all, add some more moist, rotting vegetation. Once or twice a month, turn the compost well using a shovel or pitchfork. Doing so will redistribute the decomposing organisms, which tend to migrate towards the center of the pile. Add more organic material (carbon stuff and nitrogen stuff) as you acquire it.

If it's well-tended, a compost heap should be ready within 6 months. You can tell the heap is ready if it's dark, crumbly, and has a lovely fresh-earth smell.

NOTE: People disagree about whether or not to compost cat and dog poo. Carnivore feces can contain a lot of harmful bacteria that you don't want near edible plants. Because of this, most folks will tell you to keep any and all dog/cat/wolf shit far from your compost. However, some people argue that a very active compost heap can get hot enough to kill pathogens — 160°F, to be exact. So, if you want to compost pet waste, please make sure you've got a real rager of a compost pile going. Otherwise, toss your shit elsewhere.

About Seeds

Some plants are pretty easy to grow from seed: herbs, for example, are laid-back and will most likely sprout anywhere you plant them.

Other plants are more finicky and I'll discuss them a bit later. If you're shopping for seeds, ask around first to find out if other gardeners you know favor specific brands; most experienced gardeners will have one or two brands that they find to be the most consistent and affordable. You might also try buying the same type of seed from two different sources and comparing the results of each.

For a more grassroots approach (no pun intended), check out local farmers' markets and community gardens to see if there is a seed-swapping collective or seed library in your area.

When you're planting seeds, you can either stick them straight in the ground, or you can start growing them in a small, well-controlled environment until they are big enough to be transplanted. Which path you take depends a lot on where you live: if you have good soil and consistently good weather, or if your plants are going to live in containers, direct planting is no big deal. If your area tends to get random cold snaps and weird weather patterns, as mine does, you can give your little ones a fighting chance by making sure they are strong and healthy before you put them outside. As you get more experienced as a gardener, you'll begin to cultivate (again, no pun) a sense of what kind of care to give a specific seed.

★NOTE: Always read your seed packets - they provide important information about water, sun, etc.

Direct Planting

① Always prep your beds before you plant. The soil should be moist, but not wet — too much water will prevent air circulation in the soil. Use a trowel or shovel to turn over the first few inches of earth. Doing this helps break up clumpy or compacted dirt, and it introduces air into the soil, which improves drainage.

② After you've aerated, dig a little ditch with your trowel and shift the earth you dig out to one end of the ditch. It should look like a little slide. The depth and angle of the ditch will help direct and contain water. This is especially important if you have a diversity of plants in your garden, as some plants will need more water than others.

(3) Sprinkle the seeds down into the ditch, not crowding them too much, and lightly cover them with soil. Small seeds (like herbs and lettuces) only need about ⅛" of soil on top. Bigger seeds will have to be planted farther down. Read your seed packet if you're unsure how deeply you should plant.

(4) Finally, water your seeds and mark off your rows with sticks so you can tell where they are. You should also stick a label in there somewhere.

Ideas for recycled plant labels:

★ Cut a piece of clear or translucent plastic into strips or stake shapes and write on them with permanent marker. You can use milk bottles, salad bar clamshell containers, old blister packaging, or anything else you can think of. The translucency is important, as it will let light through to delicate seedlings.

★ Snip an aluminum can into strips and bend the strips around sticks or skewers. Write on the inside of the can by pressing hard on the metal with a ballpoint pen.

★ Save all your popsicle sticks, write on them with permanent marker or waterproof grease pencil, and cover with clear nail polish.

Growing Seedlings

Many gardeners prefer to start their seeds in a controlled environment until they develop into baby plants. You can do this with the help of some soilless seed starter and a lidless egg carton. You can use good potting or garden soil too, but since seed starting mix has no dirt in it, it's free of stuff like weed seeds and harmful bacteria. It also drains well.

Seed Starting Mix

You can find these ingredients at any nursery or hardware store:

    1 part perlite

    1 part peat moss

    1 part ground sphagnum moss

Mix ingredients and keep in a bag or covered container, to keep out wayward seeds & spores.

If you don't feel like making starter mix, you can also use peat pellets, which you can buy for cheap at any nursery. Peat pellets are these amusing little pucks of peat moss that expand dramatically in water. They look like those little party favors that grow into wee face cloths with dinosaurs on them. But instead they turn into perfect little chunks of seed starter. Yippee!

+ O = boop!

① Fill each depression with damp (but not wet) starter mix that you've loosened with your hands. Tamp the soil down lightly to firm it up a bit. If you're using pellets, soak them in water until they're fully expanded, and then put one pellet in each egg cup. Make a little dent in the center of each pellet.

yeah, I can't draw egg cartons. but you could use a muffin tin too! WHATEVER.

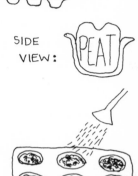

SIDE VIEW: PEAT

② Place a few seeds on each mound of dirt and cover the seeds lightly, or not so lightly, depending on the seed. Label your seeds, if you planted more than one kind.

③ Sprinkle the newly planted seeds with a little water.

④ If you like, cover the whole shebang loosely in clear plastic to create a tiny greenhouse. This will keep the seeds warm and moist. Keep the plastic on only until you see sprouts poking out. Also, make sure to let air circulate inside the plastic, to prevent molding.

⑤ Place the egg carton in a warm spot and keep an eye on it. Since the seeds are

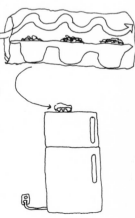

still unsprouted, sunlight is not
an issue, so don't bother putting
them near a window.

⑥ Once you start to see signs
of life, take the plastic off
and move the carton into
indirect light.

Take care of your plants
until you can see that the new
roots have reached the cardboard
of the egg carton. From there, you can either
transfer them to a bigger container that you've
filled with garden or potting soil, or you can put
them in the ground. But before you do either of
those things, consider hardening off your plants.
Maybe you are thinking ⓠ "what the hell is

HARDENING OFF?"

ⓐ This bizarre phrase refers to the process of
gradually acclimating young plants to new growing
conditions. It's sort of like getting your cat to
eat a new kind of food- in order to not piss her
off, you have to introduce the new stuff slowly
until it is familiar and comfortable for her. If
you have seedlings that you've been keeping
indoors, or in a greenhouse, introduce them to
the garden over a period of one or two weeks:

★ Begin to put your plants outside each morning. The first day, put them out only for a couple of hours; as the week progresses, leave them outside for longer and longer periods of time. You might also try switching periodically from sunny spots to shady spots.

★ Don't leave your babies at the mercy of the frosty night! If it's too cold, your plants won't get stronger — they'll just bite it. So bring them indoors or cover them if you think it's going to get chilly.

★ When you reach the point where you're leaving the seedlings out all the time, and they look strong and healthy, you can go ahead and transplant them to your garden (see "Planting Starts" on page 108). Try to transplant in the morning or evening, when the ground and air are not significantly hotter than the soil around the roots of the seedling. A smooth transplant means a healthier seedling!

Sprouting seeds

If you're trying out a seed you've never planted before, or your seeds are from a new source, you'll want to sprout them first to make sure they are viable. Sprouting is easy and beautiful, and if you're sprouting beans or alfalfa, it's also quite delicious. I also recommend sprouting to anyone who's into plant morphology, because it allows you to witness a really amazing process that's usually hidden underground.

NOTE: Sprouting does take some finesse. Show your seeds some love!

① On a tabletop or other flat surface, lay down two sheets of paper towel, one atop another. Sprinkle your seeds across one half of the resulting square.

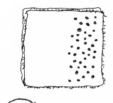

② Spread the seeds out in a single layer and fold the seed-free half of the towel over on top of the seeds.

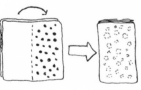

③ Fold the package twice more. Take care to keep the seeds from falling out or rolling around. This step should be done slooowly.

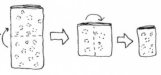

④ You should end up with a rectangle of towel about 8 layers thick. Add water to the towel a splash at a time, until all the layers are damp but not dripping wet. Try to get the towel to feel like a wet nap straight from the package.

NO DRIPS!

⑤ Place the damp towel in a plastic bag, seal it up, and slap a label on it. If you accidentally over-wet your towel, leave the bag open to let it dry out a bit.

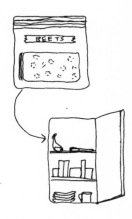

⑥ Let the sprouts sit in a cool place for about a week. Add water only if the towel is dried out; otherwise, give them their privacy. After a week is up, gently unfold the towel and- ta dah!- you've got a bunch of tittle squiggles that want planting.

⑦ Very carefully remove sprouts from the towel and plant in the ground or in a seed starter medium.

Planting Starts

Some plants, like tomatoes, produce such delicate little seeds that a lot of gardeners don't even try to start from scratch. This is why most stores and markets you go to will have an abundance of small tomato plants (called starts) that are ready to be planted in the ground. A well-stocked nursery will have lots of different starts for vegetables, fruits, herbs, and ornamentals. Using a start relieves you of the burden of coaxing a seed to sprout and develop a root structure. If you've never grown anything before, taking care of a start will help you learn how plants develop and how to keep them healthy. Another plus: ♡instant gratification♡

① Prep your beds like you're planting seeds, then dig a hole that's a little deeper than you think it should be. You're looking to bury a little of the plant's shoot under the soil. This will encourage the plant to grow new roots at the soil line.

n

n+½"

② Fill the hole up with water. Gently remove the start from its little cup and look at it's lower half. You should find a compact ball of soil and roots. Loosen the root ball with your fingers, being careful not to tear or damage the roots.

③ Place the start down into the hole and refill it with earth. Tamp the soil down firmly around the plant's stem— it will need the support. This also forms a little valley around the plant which will help direct water to the plant's roots.

When you're shopping around for starts, look for perky plants with sturdy main shoots, the thicker the better. Many lateral stems are also a good sign. Pass on plants that are super leggy,* are drooping over, or have signs of insect damage. If you like, you can hold the plant on its side and tug off the container to check the roots. Look for a root ball that's sizable, but does not make a tight basket around the inside of the container. Root-bound plants are difficult to transplant and will not grow very well.

* leggy = very long main shoot with few lateral stems

Watering

Misinformed watering is a really effective way to kill your plants. I feel like a lot of folks think that if they let their plants get dry their whole garden will, like, explode or melt or something. Ok, so nobody thinks that, but still, there's a lot of anxiety about the possibility of underwatering. The truth is that overwatering your plants can be just as bad for them, and damn wasteful to boot. So, here are some tips for proper watering:

• Water your plants whenever the soil is dry 1-3" below the surface, or if the plant looks withered. **Stick your finger** in the dirt to check dryness

• The best time to water is early morning or late afternoon. Daytime is just too hot – most of the water will just evaporate. Watering at night is usually ok, but it can sometimes put your plants at risk for mold.

• A thorough watering once or twice a week is almost always preferable to daily sprinkling. The exception to this is small seedlings, which need constant moisture. Watering deeply, but less often, will encourage plants to grow deep roots in order to search for moisture. Daily watering is unlikely to seep below the first few inches of soil, and the plants in turn will develop shallow, less stable roots.

• If you see flabby, yellowed leaves, you are overwatering.

fertilizing

I guess we'll call it the way of the civilized world: because vegetables as we know them have been cultivated for hundreds of years, most of them can no longer grow in regular garden soil. They're just used to being pampered. So even if you have naturally good soil and good seeds, you might need some fertilizer. Shopping for fertilizer is intimidating: you can choose either neon blue chemical powder or organic fertilizers like ground up fish. Both of these can seem bizarre and confusing to a novice gardener. Luckily, unless you have a very large operation underway, you won't have to deal with all that. There are lots of effective, sustainable fertilizers that can be had for next to no money. But first, some science.

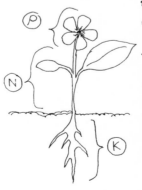

Plants need three main nutrients: nitrogen, phosphorous, + potassium. Nitrogen is essential in the formation of leaves and shoots, phosphorous encourages flowering, and potassium (potash) is a root stimulant. A good garden will need all three of these, plus a few trace nutrients like calcium and magnesium. Nitrogen, in its soluble form, is gobbled up by vegetables and is leached easily from the soil by rain or irrigation; if you live in a rainy climate or you water a lot, your garden might need a nitrogen boost more often. Other nutrients, especially potash + trace minerals, stick around a lot longer. Unless your garden is under constant torrential downpour (at which point an indoor garden is probably a good idea), you won't need to add these nutrients more than once or twice a year.

And now... we fertilize!

• <u>Compost</u>, your favorite thing in the world, is a fantastic fertilizer! Make sure your heap contains stuff like grass clippings, wood ashes, egg shells, used coffee grounds, and if you can get it, kelp and cow or horse manure. These materials make a very rich, balanced fertilizer. When your compost is totally decomposed, work it into your soil, a few pounds of compost per square foot of earth. This is best done in the fall when you're preparing your beds for winter, because the soil will settle over the cold months and the nutrients will be redistributed. Also make sure to put some 'post in the bottom of the holes you dig while transplanting seedlings or starts. You should also include a good amount of compost in any mix you're using to grow plants in containers.

A note about manure, and nitrogen in general: it might seem like a good idea to cut out the middleman and spread manure right on your beds, but it's really not. Manure and other really rich sources of nitrogen need to be aged and rotted through before they become usable, and that's why we compost them first. If you overfertilize by putting a buttload (pun totally intended) of manure on your beds, the nitrogen can actually scorch your plants. So, if you notice that the leaves in your garden look burned, even if they're not in direct sunlight, lay off the fertilizer, ok?

Manure tea: is easy to make. Just add a few handfuls of aged manure (available at nurseries) to a pail of water, let it sit around for an afternoon and use it to water new transplants or on plants that look wimpy, especially leafy greens.

Alfalfa tea: You can get alfalfa meal or pellets at the nursery. Put 10 or so double handfuls of alfalfa in a large, lidded container like a trash bin. Fill the bin mostly full of water, stir it with a big stick, lid it and leave it. Stir this once a day or so for 3-4 days or until it starts to smell truly disgusting. When that happens, it's ready! Scoop out some tea with a watering can and sprinkle onto soil that you've already irrigated with plain water. Keep your alfalfa tea in a sunny spot and keep it covered whenever you're not stirring. It really is nasty-smelling, but that goes away after a while.

Staking & Trellising

If you're growing tomatoes, peppers, and the like, you're gonna need to overcome your fear of chicken wire (I know: it pokes!) and support those suckers. Viney plants like nightshades tend to have weak stems and heavy fruits. Once those fruits mature, they're liable to cause the plant to topple in bad weather and/or crush smaller plants. Plus, once the fruits are on the ground, the will most likely burst, rot, or invite hordes of crawling insects. To prevent this, support plant stems with a few stakes, or better yet, a cage. These are easy to make: just bend a rectangle of chicken wire (wear gloves!) into a cylinder and plop it over young plants. DONE!

Peas, beans and other vines need support too, but you've got tons more options:

in a tepee!

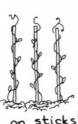

on sticks!

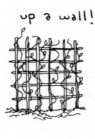

up a wall!

in an arbor!

Vines climb stuff naturally, so to train peas and beans to grow on a support, you really just need to show them where it is. Young plants will start to sprout little tendrils that are quite strong: just wrap these early tendrils around your chosen support, and the vine will start growing up the support. Not only does this add a lovely vertical element to your garden, it makes peas and beans easier to pick! And bean tepees make the best forts ever.

★ If you have older* varieties of corn growing, try training pole beans to grow around the stalks! This is part of the "3 Sisters Garden" used by Native American tribes in the eastern part of North America. The other sister is squash, by the way.   * older: stronger than newer hybrids

If you're gardening in a small space, try trellising other plants like squashes, cucumbers, raspberries, zucchini and eggplant. You can get creative here, just remember that a heavier plant will need a sturdier support. To keep fruits in place on the trellis, try securing the stems to the trellis with twine or cut-up pantyhose. Tie loosely to give the plant room to grow.

maintaining your Garden

So, you've got leaves unfurling and your pea vines are spitting tendrils everywhere. Here is what to do to make sure your garden doesn't bite it:

Weeding

I know it sucks. I know it makes you uncomfortable to try and control what Nature graciously provides. But you gotta do it: if you don't, non-native noxious weeds will strangle your vegetables! *I am not kidding.* Keep your garden organized and you'll be able to spot young weeds and get them out before they produce seeds. If you can't get their roots out because they're too close to your veggies, cut them off at ground level and keep cutting them back until they're dead. And remember that a lot of weeds can be used medicinally, so once you get that plantain out of your garden, dry it and use it in a salve!

Thinning

As your vegetables come up, you'll probably have a few rows that are a little too crowded. Go over these rows and pick out a few of the scrawny-looking seedlings to give the healthy plants more room. Larger plants, like pumpkins and eggplants, will need more room between plants than, for example, snow peas. Plants won't grow if they don't have room, so give them their space!

<u>Pruning</u> - some plants, like tomatoes, ripen best in the sunshine. Snip off any leaves that are throwing shade over your fruits.

If you're growing herbs, they'll need to be pruned also. This will keep them growing outwards, rather than upwards. Pruning will also delay flowering, which can cause herb leaves to taste bitter. To trim plants, pinch off the tops of the stalks on a regular basis. They love it!

<u>Preparing for Winter</u> - Even if you planted a garden full of annuals, you'll probably be interested in keeping your soil viable until the next planting. There a couple of ways to do this.

① Start early and till your soil in the fall, after you harvest. Work in compost and other amendments, and cover with a layer of mulch to protect the topsoil.

② If you have any perennials planted, they'll live underground through the winter. Pick off any old stems or leaves on top of the soil, and add a layer of mulch to keep roots warm.

③ Plant a cover crop! A cover crop will maintain soil integrity, keep weeds from germinating, and, in the spring, it can be dug into the earth to enrich the soil. Grains like rye and winter wheat are popular cover crops. If you're a serious DIYer, you can even harvest your cover crop!

PEST CONTROL

Regardless of how urban your garden might be, it's still part of an ecosystem that includes bugs, deer, birds, and other animals that will enjoy eating the fruits of your labor. They're a royal pain, to be sure, but try to remember that these creatures are just doing what they do. Try not to take it personally! Instead of directing your malice towards them, try to control intruders without killing them. I think it's worth it, even though it's a bit more work. This section will focus on using preventative measures whenever possible, to keep pests out of your garden in the first place. Let's work big to small:

• Deer can usually be kept out with a good fence. You can either install a fence around your whole yard, or make a small garden enclosure out of chicken wire. You can also try gathering human hair clippings, stuffing them in the toes of some old nylons, and hanging them around the perimeter of their garden. Deer think you reek and will avoid anyplace that smells like people.

• Dig out a shallow trench and <u>then</u> install your fence, so part of it is underground; it will guard against rabbits. You can also try scattering human hair around your garden, placing a few vinegar-soaked corncobs in between plants, or sprinkling some red pepper flakes over the dirt. If you like bunnies but don't want them eating your lettuce, plant some clover in another part of your yard - it's one of their favorite foods.

· To keep cats from digging in your yard, take a few handfuls of thin sticks or skewers and stick them in the dirt at an angle. The sticks will make it so kitties won't be able to  find a clear space to squat in. Two more ideas: ① Plant a border of lemon thyme or lemon balm (cats don't like citrus); ② divert their attention with a plot of catnip elsewhere in your yard.

· Moles don't eat veggies, but they will uproot them in the course of their digging. To prevent this, plant vegetables in a raised bed, lined at the bottom with some wire mesh.

· Some light netting draped over vegetables (or arced over them with half hoops) will keep birds from eating fruits and scratching in the ground. A nice distracting bird feeder can also help.

BUGS!

Alas, you cannot simply build a tiny fence to keep bugs out of your yard. But! There are some ways to control them without resorting to crop dusting. Specific bugs might need specialized care, but here are the basics:

· Know your bug before you launch an attack. A lot of insects are a) just minding their own and not actually hurting your garden, b) only there short-term and will happily leave on their own,

c) actually beneficial to your garden. Focus your energy on bugs that you know are hurting your plants, especially if they're non-native.

• A diverse, healthy garden will attract far fewer pests than an unkempt monoculture. Plant a lot of different veggies, don't overwater, and if your plants die, don't leave their corpses lying around.

• Attract beneficial bug-eaters, like ladybugs, praying mantis, green lacewings, and bats. You can also buy ladybugs and houses for bats. To attract ladybugs, plant umbrella-shaped plants like fennel, dill, and cilantro.

• Strong smelling plants like mint, garlic and rosemary will repel and confuse insects.

• If you find bugs on your plants, a strong spray from a hose will knock them off. Bigger ones (like slugs) can be picked off by hand and dropped into a bucket of soapy water (violent, I know. I'm sorry).

• Add a few tablespoons of castile soap (mint-scented, if you have it) to a gallon of water and pour some in a spray bottle. Spray on bugs you find on indoor or outdoor plants. Make sure you rinse veggies before you eat them!

• Plant a row of sacrificial plants (radishes are good) around your garden to distract bugs from more precious crops

this here's a pot!
indoor + container gardening

I'm going to assume that some of you out there are, like me, apartment dwellers. It has been years since I had my own yard; I spend a lot of time daydreaming about hammocks. Limited outdoor space is a part of the urban landscape — but that doesn't mean it should keep you from growing food! Luckily, container gardening is an option for almost everyone, and tons of fruits + veggies grow well in containers. Witness the ABUNDANCE!:

lettuces
cabbage beets garlic
spring onions tomatoes carrots peppers strawberries
radishes herbs
anything that says "dwarf," "bush" or "compact" on the label

And now, the basics: you need a pot. Does it need to be a nice pot, or even a pot-shaped pot? Hell no! Pretty much any container that can hold soil, not rot away, and drain excess water can function as a planter. Depending on what plant you're growing, coffee cans, baskets, windowboxes, old boots, wooden crates, buckets, jugs and big sacks can all be utilized, as well as a host of other junk. Just make sure you can put at least two ½" drainage holes in the bottom. Also, choose a bigger container than you think you'll need — it needs to be big enough to accomodate a mature root system and wide enough so that the weight of the plant won't cause it to topple. Once you've got a sufficient container, line the base with newspaper to prevent soil erosion.

Secondly, dirt. Commercial potting soil is usually made of peat and other light, quick-draining stuff. These materials are weed-and disease-free, and they keep plants from getting waterlogged. The DIY version of potting soil is compost, or compost mixed with a bit of sand - check your seed packets to see if your seeds like sand in their soil. You yardless folks- check your local community garden to see if you can score some free compost.

Seeds for container gardens can be sprouted first or planted directly in their new home. Once you have some leaves sprouting, move the pot (or whatever) to the sunniest part of your house. Fruiting plants, like tomatoes, are especially greedy for sun. If you find that the sunniest part of your home = too much sun, you can move them. Because pots are awesome.

Since potting soil drains so quickly, container gardens need to be watered and fertilized more often than in-ground gardens. Water whenever the soil is dry under the surface, but not if only the first ½ inch or so is dry. If your plants need a boost, give them manure tea once in a while.

Resources and further reading

♡= favorites

General Herbal Health & First Aid

The Green Pharmacy, by James A Duke, PhD
(Rodale Books, 1999)

♡The Backyard Medicine Chest, by Douglas Schar
(Elliot & Clark, 1995) ♡

Prescription for Nutritional Healing, by Phyllis
♡ Balch (Avery, 2006)

Cat's Claw♡Herbal, by Heron (self-published)*

Herbal Gynecology

♡Hot Pantz: Do it Yourself Gynecology, by Isabelle
Gauthier and Lisa Vinebaum (self-published)*

Take Back Your Life: A Wimmin's Guide to Alternative
Health Care, by Alicia non Grata (originally
published by Profane Existence Collective)*

Nontoxic Cleaning and Body Care

♡Better Basics for the Home, by♡Annie Berthold-
Bond (Three Rivers Press, 1999)

The Naturally Clean Home, by Karyn Siegel Maier
(Storey Publishing LLC, 1999)

Herbal Homekeeping, by Sandy Maine
(Interweave Press, 1999)

*Available from Microcosm, www.microcosmpublishing.com

Clean House Clean Planet, by Karen Logan
(Pocket, 1997)

Vim and Vinegar!, by Melodie Moore
(Harper Paperbacks, 1997)

Baking Soda Bonanza!, by Peter E. Ciullo
(Harper Perennial, 1995)

Gardening

♡
Compost This Zine, by Liz Defiance (self-published)
♡
Home Composting Made Easy (self-published) *

Basic Gardening, by Louise Carter
(Fulcrum Publishing, 1995)

The Organic Suburbanite, by Warren Schultz
(Rodale Books, 2001)

Dave's Garden - www.davesgarden.com
-A very active online community with tons of
articles about all types of gardening

All Around DIY Amazingness

♡
Making Stuff and Doing Things, collected by
Kyle Bravo ♡(Microcosm Publishing, 2005)

Microcosm Publishing is Portland's most diversified publishing house and distributor with a focus on the colorful, authentic, and empowering. Our books and zines have put your power in your hands since 1996, equipping readers to make positive changes in their lives and in the world around them. Microcosm emphasizes skill-building, showing hidden histories, and fostering creativity through challenging conventional publishing wisdom with books and bookettes about DIY skills, food, bicycling, gender, self-care, and social justice. What was once a distro and record label was started by Joe Biel in his bedroom and has become among the oldest independent publishing houses in Portland, OR. We are a politically moderate, centrist publisher in a world that has inched to the right for the past 80 years.

Global labor conditions are bad, and our roots in industrial Cleveland in the 70s and 80s makes us appreciate the need to treat workers right. Therefore, our books are MADE IN THE USA and printed on post-consumer paper.

SUBSCRIBE TO EVERYTHING WE PUBLISH!

Do you love what Microcosm publishes?

Do you want us to publish more great stuff?

Would you like to receive each new title as it's published?

Subscribe as a BFF to our new titles and we'll mail them all to you as they are released!

$10-30/mo, pay what you can afford. Include your t-shirt size and your birthday for a possible surprise!

microcosmpublishing.com/bff

...AND HELP US GROW YOUR SMALL WORLD!

Other books about the House & Home Revolution:

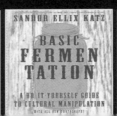